D0904282

Women in Saudi Arabia

B.R.O.E. LIBRARY
950 N. Upon Ave.
Ba̲s̲ ... s̲
(817) 364-3570

WOMEN IN SAUDI ARABIA

Ideology and Behavior Among the Elite

SORAYA ALTORKI

B. B. C. F. LIBRARY
Boston, MA

COLUMBIA UNIVERSITY PRESS
New York

Library of Congress Cataloging in Publication Data

Altorki, Soraya.
Women in Saudi Arabia.

Bibliography: p.
Includes index.
1. Women—Saudi Arabia—Jiddah—History.
2. Family—Saudi Arabia—Jiddah—History.   3. Jiddah
(Saudi Arabia)—Social conditions.   4. Elite (Social
sciences)—Saudi Arabia—Jiddah—History.   I. Title.
HQ1730.A66   1986   305.4'09538   85-14966
ISBN   0-231-06182-X (alk. paper)
ISBN 0-231-06183-8 (pbk.)

Columbia University Press
New York   Guildford, Surrey
Copyright © 1986 Columbia University Press
All rights reserved

Printed in the United States of America
p 10 9 8 7 6 5 4 3 2
c 10 9 8 7 6 5 4 3 2

To the Memory of My Father
and
To the Memory of My Husband

Contents

Acknowledgments

MANY FRIENDS and colleagues have encouraged this work in its various stages, and I would like to thank them all. I especially would like to thank Professor Janet Abu Lughod, Professor Jack Potter, and Dr. Sulamith Heins Potter, all three of whom took valuable time from their busy schedules to read a later draft of this book and made incisive comments that guided its final progress. My special thanks also to Professor Nels Johnson, whose suggestions were crucial to the analytical thrust of this work.

I am happy to acknowledge the support given me by Professor Cynthia Nelson in arranging for my leave of absence from American University in Cairo during 1983–1984 and for her overall encouragement of my work. My appreciation to Ms. Wafa Mahrous, who patiently and cheerfully waded through my illegible handwriting to type the major part of the first draft. Additional thanks go to Ms. Nadia Taher for her indispensable moral support and practical assistance as the research progressed. I also gratefully acknowledge the Middle East Research Institute of the University of Pennsylvania (where I was a fellow for the second semester of 1983–1984) for the use of their facilities and the very helpful assistance of their staff. My gratitude is due Dr. Shams 'Inati for allowing me to sound out my ideas on her and kindly nudging me along. My special thanks to Karen Mitchell for a thorough copyediting job.

Finally, my particular thanks go to my brother. His sensitivity and profound knowledge of the culture were invaluable to my work and to my adjustment in my society. His tolerance, encouragement, and firm belief in women's education sustained me through the hardest moments in the field.

A Note on Transliteration

THE TRANSLITERATION of Arabic terms follows the usage in Hans Wehr, *A Dictionary of Modern Written Arabic*, edited by J. Milton Cowan (Ithaca, N.Y.: Cornell University Press, 1961) and that utilized in the Library of Congress system. Although a number of words have colloquial forms (for example, *baqshish* has often been transliterated in the colloquial, *bakshish*) and some place names have familiar spellings (for example, Mecca and Medina rather than Macca and Madina). I felt that for the sake of consistency the classical Arabic form should be transliterated in the text. The diacritical marks used are an apostrophe "ʼ" for the glottal stop (*hamzah*) and the turned comma "ʻ" for the *ʻayn*.

Women in Saudi Arabia

CHAPTER ONE

THE CITY AND THE PEOPLE

THIS IS A STUDY of continuity and change among elite domestic groups in Jiddah, Saudi Arabia. To understand these changes, I compare the behavior and ideology of three generations of that city's prominent families, which are defined in terms of important historical events. Focusing on the dynamics of role relationships within and among families, I hope to reduce the level of abstraction common to many ethnographic community studies. Too often, studies dealing with the Middle East have either dealt with the reconstruction of conditions in earlier centuries, or else they have portrayed current conditions against the background of events in the distant past.

I hope that the present work provides an understanding of social change in domestic groups in Middle Eastern society. The long duration of fieldwork (undertaken in 1971–1973, 1974–1976, and 1976–1984) captures a span of changes for the community as a whole. Thus, the study is able to compare recent trends with conditions in the early years of the rule of Ibn Sa'ud (d. 1953) and the establishment of the Kingdom of Saudi Arabia.

At Home in the Field

Fieldwork for this study extended over several years. Beginning in June 1971, an eighteen-month period was followed by another twenty months in 1974–1976, during which I taught at King 'Abd al-'Aziz University in Jiddah. After that, and until 1984, I made regular and shorter visits to the city and kept up with most of the families still residing there.

When I decided to do fieldwork in my own society, I was unaware

of the very special problems that such research entails.[1] I was excited about the possibility of combining my training as an anthropologist with my native experience in order to reach a deeper
understanding of my own culture than a foreign ethnographer
could hope to achieve. I soon discovered, however, that although I
was raised in a Saudi Arabian family, my long years of residence
abroad had made me somewhat of a stranger to my own culture.

Other problems were more critical. Little did I anticipate the frustrations that my status as an unmarried woman would impose on
my fieldwork. These ranged from restrictions on my movements to
severe curtailment of interaction with other people. Yet, the initial
frustrations turned out to have unexpected rewards: I was a conscious witness to my own resocialization as an Arab woman,
and thus I learned many aspects of this role in the best manner
possible. I became what can best be described as an observant
participant.

My decision to study family life was not a matter of choice so
much as a consequence of the field situation. The domestic culture
of urban families was for me the most accessible sphere of social
relations. It also happens to be the least accessible for foreign re-
searchers, especially if they are men.

Although as a native I did not find my work slowed by any bu-
reaucratic red tape, I had to face other difficulties. For example, I
had no freedom to move in public on my own, and challenging any
norms of conduct would have jeopardized my relationships with
the families I had decided to study. Had I not conformed, I would
have risked being ostracized and having my research terminated.
Persistently, if slowly, I achieved a precarious balance of roles that
allowed the mobility to do my research as well as to be accepted
and taken seriously. This process gave me an excellent opportunity
to learn the norms of appropriate behavior and experience their
constraints.

These problems were further compounded by the fact that Saudi
Arabia represents virtual *terra incognita* for social science research.
Saudi Arabian society has not been studied by many social scien-
tists. Certainly, urban Saudi Arabia, though physically more accessible than the desert country, captured less of the interest of
early Western travelers, who were more fascinated by the nomad

and his camel. Thus few studies focused on urban life (see Burton 1855; Hurgronje 1888–89).

In addition, the families that I worked with form closed groups whose confidence even I could gain only through patient approaches along lines of friendship. Although generous hospitality is highly valued behavior, there remain degrees of formality that the families must always maintain vis-à-vis the rest of the community. Only with considerable caution can a nonmember see their lives as they live them, rather than as these families want the rest of the community to know them. For example, it takes a long time, coupled with intensive interaction, before people allow a friend to move in their house beyond the façade of formality shown to any *ajanib*. This expression literally means foreigners, but it also refers to friends with whom a measure of social distance is observed. Indeed, it took between six and eight months before I could develop a relationship of trust with the families and deepen the friendships that made close observation of their daily lives possible to such a degree that my presence was more or less ignored. Of the thirteen families I studied, I was able to overcome barriers of formality with only eight.

There was another barrier that I had to overcome: the image which the community had of me. My being a woman who had been educated abroad, even beyond college, made the women—particularly the older generation—cautious in discussing their beliefs and practices with me. Repeatedly, they evaded my questions, remaining quiet or even giving me different views from those they actually held. Behind their maneuvers was a disturbing apprehension that, because of my education, I would judge them as ignorant and as belonging to another era. Such fears have their roots in the changes that the society is undergoing, where the members of the older generation find some of their beliefs and practices, especially religious ideas, criticized or redefined.

The obvious advantages that I had, as a native anthropologist, were further diminished by an attitude on the part of my informants that I ought to know my culture. For example, when I was interviewing women on basic religious rituals, I found that my questions shocked them. Smilingly, one informant asked, "Are you not ashamed that you do not know how to pray at your age? How can you not know these things? What, then, do they teach you abroad?" I had great difficulties in getting data on aspects of the culture I was expected to know. Yet, it was precisely this procedure that allowed me to learn the "cultural repertoire" that I was expected to have, notwithstanding my absence abroad. I discovered that the best strategy of exploration was to confess my ignorance and ask them to teach me again to be a Muslim Saudi woman.

Thus, my ignorance of the culture, as a result of not having lived in the society for any length of time (until the period of fieldwork) since the age of six, made it possible for me to learn about the culture and not to take much of it for granted. Yet, this conscious socialization did not come to me as a foreigner, but as a member with the task of abiding by the norms she studied. There were advantages to this role.

As a woman, I was able to explore the domestic scene in a way no male anthropologist ever could. On the other hand, the cultural limitations placed on my relation to the world of men did present some obstacles to my study. Since domestic groups were the only field of social relations accessible to me as an unmarried woman, most of the data was gathered from women. I could not gather data about the men in these families as they related to other men in friendship networks, in business activities, and in daily interaction in the public world. Within the household, men's gatherings, especially of the older generation and to an extent in the younger generation, were exclusively male affairs. Even in mixed gatherings men and women maintained decorous distance, and an invisible barrier segregated the conversations of the sexes. Occasionally, the barrier would be crossed by a conventional topic of general concern (for example, health, children's schooling, vacations, etc.). Only when the gathering included a "close friend" or an individual with whom interaction was frequent did men and women talk with one another more freely.

Fortunately, this limitation in the data was inconsequential for activities which took place within the house. The book is limited in what it can say about the world of men as they relate to one another in the public sphere, where men, and not women, are the principal social actors. This is not to say that I remained ignorant of the world of men. Where it concerns the younger generation, I used my long absence from my society as a legitimate excuse for assuming a certain freedom of interaction with the men that they would not have tolerated from an unmarried woman who had grown up in the society.

During the several months of fieldwork, I lived with relatives and gathered my data through observation of behavior and intensive interviewing. I collected case histories of marriage, divorce, naming, gift exchanges, friendship relations, and residence patterns. Some of the interviews were conducted with only one or two informants present. Other interviews took place in the presence of women of different age groups. This method provided some control on the influence of age differences on knowledge and opinions expressed. For example, what older illiterate women told me about certain religious beliefs and rituals probably differs from what they would have said in the presence of their literate daughters and daughters-in-law. Similarly, some of the views expressed by the young women could not be voiced in the presence of their mothers or mothers-in-law.

I also visited and observed nonelite families, many of which I met in the houses of the elite. Economically, these were people either of modest means (who, as such, qualified as recipients of alms) or they were financially comfortable and had a more egalitarian relationship to the elite. The former, of course, were in a dependency relationship with the elite. Some were friends who came on frequent visits and offered their services and assistance when needed. Almost all these would recieve the *zakat* (religious charity tax) from the elite during the month of Ramadan. On the other hand, there were those who were economically well off, some even wealthier than the members of the elite but who lacked elite status because they did not possess some of the other status determinants described below.

The Setting: Jiddah

In this section I will give a brief history of the development of the city of Jiddah from the seventh century to the present, highlighting its unique role as contact point for the north of the peninsula with the external world; the consequent heterogeneity of its population; the economic base for the city; the circumstances that led to the first prolonged contact the families of this study had with a society other than their own; and finally, the demographic concepts that the people use to describe the population of the city.

The oldest location for the city of Jiddah, resting on the shores of the Red Sea and for many years the kingdom's largest, dates back to the time of the caliph 'Uthman ibn 'Affan (r. 642–656). Although some date it to pre-Islamic times,[2] more often the caliph 'Uthman is associated with its establishment.[3] Since those times the site on the Red Sea has grown slowly, fluctuating between periods of relative prosperity and long periods of setbacks, when both the size of the city and its population dwindled.

Jiddah's strategic location, on the trade routes from India in the east and Yemen and Ethiopia to the south, was one of the main reasons for its growth. Its location, when combined with political stability, brought Jiddah prosperity. For example, under Ayyubid rule in Egypt (1169–1260), Salah al-Din freed the Red Sea from the Crusaders and placed its trade firmly in Muslim hands. Thus, the trade routes linking East and West passed through Jiddah and the competing port of 'Aydhab on the opposite shore of the Red Sea.[4]

Obviously, competition with other seaports reduced the benefits from trade, but the pilgrimage (*hajj*) provided another main activity that improved the economic conditions of the city. Located in the Hijaz (the western province of present-day Saudi Arabia, and the home of Macca and Madina), Jiddah was and still is the main port of entry for the pilgrimage. Rival ports, such as Yanbu', near Madina, were closer to Egypt, the source of many pilgrims, and so deflected some of the revenues from the pilgrimage, but they never were on a par with Jiddah. Among the reasons for this is that Jiddah is blessed with a natural harbor, protected by a reef that provides shelter from wind and storm.

Despite these conditions, Jiddah's prosperity was not proportionate with its location and physical features, for two main reasons. First, the pilgrimage sometimes proceeded on land and, while it passed by Jiddah, it did not use the port. For example, during Fatimid rule (969–1169) the pilgrimage route crossed from Suez and 'Aydhab to Jiddah.[5] During the Ayyubid period that followed, the more frequent route bypassed Jiddah by crossing to 'Aqabah in the north and proceeded by land to Macca and Madina. This continued until 1883, when, under Ottoman rule, the Suez-Jiddah route saw the regular stream of pilgrimage. It was about that time that pilgrims from India, who earlier had come on land via Iran or by sailboat, now came in large ships from ports near Bombay.[6]

The second main reason for Jiddah's lagging prosperity was the political instability and disorder resulting from the overall conditions in the Muslim empire and the power struggles among the indigenous Amirs, stimulated by external interest from Baghdad, Egypt, Yemen, and Turkey. These conditions reduced trade and cut down the flow of pilgrims to the Hijaz, periodically plunging its cities into economic decline and general disarray. Examples of this are found throughout the long historical period from 'Abbasid rule (750–1258) to the twentieth century.

With Ottoman rule, which extended to the Hijaz in 1517, began the power struggle relevant to understanding the modern period in this region. A *wali*, or Ottoman representative, was posted to Jiddah, and Turkish garrisons were established in Macca and Madina, as well. Competing with the Ottoman Turks at times and accepting nominal or actual suzerainty at other times was the local Ashraf dynasty, which administered the government with an Amir in Macca and an appointed representative in Jiddah.[7]

This Arab-Ottoman competition was challenged in the north by Ibn Sa'ud who, in July 1924, began his long bid for control of the Hijaz. The Ashraf were defeated in Taif in a memorable battle in September of that year. Ashraf rule was shaken at its capital, Macca, whereupon the civilian population fled in fear to the city of Jiddah. In an attempt to appease Ibn Sa'ud, leaders from Jiddah and Macca pressured Husayn, the leader of the Ashraf, to abdicate in favor of his son 'Ali, who now took Jiddah to be his new capital. These leaders formed the National Hijazi Party to help meet the national crisis.[8] So, when Ibn Sa'ud's forces advanced from Taif weeks after its fall, they encountered almost no resistance in Macca and quickly established their control over the most sacred city in the Muslim world. Then began the long siege of Jiddah, which precipitated the first wave of emigration experienced by families included in this study. Many went to India, the Sudan, Egypt, and Eritrea. They settled in these areas for periods of 12–16 months, not returning home until Ibn Saʻud had entered Jiddah (December 1925) and established himself King of the Hijaz in January 1926.

Because of its strategic location and the commercial activity it generated, Jiddah remained the major city in the peninsula in the early years of the present Saudi dynasty. As such, it was the actual, if not the formal, seat of the government for all the Hijaz and the main beneficiary of the relative prosperity ushered in by the stability of Saudi rule. Equally important at this time was the role Jiddah played as the link between the desert interior and the world outside.

The cosmopolitan nature of the city and its heterogeneous population gave Jiddah a combination unique in the early days of the kingdom. A long mercantile tradition, varied life-styles and cultures of the city population, and the regular contact with non-Muslims through the port made for a relatively open attitude to the world outside and a wider awareness of alternatives. All these factors made Jiddah especially suited to benefit from the intensifying contact with the outside world which the drilling of oil, beginning in 1935, had brought to the country. Thus, it is not surprising that, despite the shift of the capital to Riyadh in 1952–1953 and the abrupt move there of the government departments, Jiddah continued to prosper.

Oil brought in revenues dramatically greater than in previous historical periods, when the two main sources of wealth had been the pilgrimage and taxes from the port. The young men, who were better trained than their parents, were in a better position to profit from the new economic opportunities. Consequently, it was not uncommon for these men to be wealthier than their parents. But even before oil, trade and the pilgrimage had given Jiddah a viable economic base, to which oil revenues then brought boom and prosperity. One ought to be aware of the fact, then, that it is only with the last decade, when the building of Riyadh was completed, that Jiddah was reduced to the second largest city in the kingdom.

Despite Riyadh's preeminence, many informants, especially businessmen, perceive that Jiddah remains the biggest city. As one such man put it, "it is not the seat of government, it is not where the big money is, but its people have something that makes all businessmen, especially foreigners, prefer dealing with them. Everyone wants to come to Jiddah if he can."

There is no doubt that Jiddah has a longer history of contact with the outside world than other Arabian towns and an enduring pattern of mercantile relations unknown to the interior of the peninsula. It is through Jiddah that contact with the West has been made through trade, and it is in Jiddah that the first foreign diplomatic representation began in 1801 with the opening of the British Consulate, followed later by French and Russian consulates.[9] It is also in Jiddah that leading men opened the first formal school in 1905.[10] By 1951 there were 210 schools in the kingdom, and by 1954 the Ministry of Education, which systematized the educational institution and opened more schools throughout the country, was formed. Girls' schools, however, did not open until 1960. In 1984, Jiddah had a total of 182 schools for boys and 154 schools for girls. There are also a number of training institutes for girls and boys. The young King 'Abd al-'Aziz University was opened by 1967. Again, interestingly enough, the initiative was taken by leading men in the city who pooled their efforts to give Jiddah its first institution of higher learning. Later, this became a state university. Jiddah also had the first bank, hospital, and airport in the kingdom. The first port, Jiddah remains the most important entry to the Hijaz. With 42 berths, the port handles up to 19 million tons of cargo each year, amounting to 50 percent of all imports into the kingdom.

Given this history of exposure, it is not surprising that Jiddah has one of the most heterogeneous populations in the kingdom. Over many years the local population has been increased by numbers of migrants who settled in the main cities of the Hijaz. According to a local historian, Siba'i, migration to the Hijaz occurred for purposes of trade and scholarly pursuit of the religious sciences in Macca, in addition to the specific historical conditions that pushed migrants out of their native homes to find sanctuary in the sacred cities of the Hijaz. Migrants arrived from Morocco, Syria, Egypt (especially after the expedition to Macca by the Pasha of Egypt, Muhammad 'Ali, in 1811–1818), and to a lesser degree from Iraq, Iran, and parts of Africa. Turks also intermarried and stayed, but other Asians, such as Indians, Indonesians, Malay, and Bukhari, increased in numbers only when transportation improved by the turn of this century. The greatest numbers, however, have come from Hadramawt and Yemen, and also Najd—though the latter did not increase in number until after Saudi rule was established over the Hijaz. In addition to these various ethnic groups, Jiddah's population includes *badu* (nomads) from some major tribes such as Harb, who settled down to engage in fishing; and others, such as Bani Malik, who mainly work as brokers for the sale of sheep and the wholesale of vegetables and fruits from Taif. The boost to the economy after Saudi Arabia went "on stream" with oil added to the ethnic diversity of the city by attracting Lebanese, Syrians, Pakistanis, Jordanians, and Iraqis. They are predominantly engaged as teachers in primary and secondary schools, as skilled laborers, as physicians, chemists, engineers, contractors, nurses, and businessmen. Within the last decade, the unprecedented growth of oil revenues brought foreign labor, mostly non-Arab and non-Muslim, to all the major cities in the kingdom except the holy cities of Macca and Madina. Today, the streets of Jiddah show a visible variety of nationalities, and Saudis jokingly refer to their own numbers as being few and far between.

The most recent census was taken in 1974, and Jiddah's population was estimated to be 558,528. It includes other Arab communities of Lebanese, Jordanians, Syrians, Palestinians, and Egyptians as well as non-Arabs. They work in skilled professions, such as medicine, teaching, engineering, and specialized crafts. There are, in addition, foreign residents from embassies and companies (Japanese, American, French, German, English, and Italian) who are mainly involved in construction.

The largest segment of Jiddah's native population refer to themselves and are referred to by others as *ahl al-balad*. The literal meaning is "people of the country," but the term is used by the *ahl al-balad* themselves to differentiate themselves from the foreign community, from recent immigrants, and also from the Bedouin tribes who have settled—as far back as the oldest informant can remember—in what were the outskirts of the city. As a demographic concept, *ahl al-balad* establishes fluid boundaries. For example, when men speak of *ahl al-balad* they mean primarily Hijazis, but may also include other Saudis. Depending on the social context the concept defines wider or narrower boundaries of identification. In the restricted use it excludes other Hijazis—for example, Bedouins—and in its wide use it may include "all the people of the land," differentiating them from other nationalities including other Arabs living in Jiddah or in the kingdom. This latter meaning, however, is recent and is related to the influx of other Arabs and foreigners which the economic boom brought to the kingdom. Older-generation and middle-generation women usually use the term in its narrower sense, while men and younger-generation women with some schooling often use the term in its wider sense. Hence the semantic variation of *ahl al-balad* tends to be limited to men and younger-generation women.

As a cultural concept *ahl al-balad* classifies individuals and families who share the following characteristics. First, they are all Muslims, although their origin might be Indian, Indonesian, Syrian, Iraqi, Egyptian, Persian, Hadramawti, or Yemeni, as well as the indigenous Hijazis. Second, their families have lived in Jiddah for at least 80 to 100 years. Third, they are not *badu*. While length of residence is an important criterion by which the *ahl al-balad* set themselves apart from the recent immigrants to the city, it is not an exclusive aspect, since the urban *badu* do not belong to this group. And finally, they are not connected to the other regions of the peninsula. Until recently, the Najdites were not considered by the people, nor did they consider themselves, *ahl al-balad*. Instead, they saw themselves as Najdites (people from Najd) or Shuruq (from *sharq*, meaning east, and denoting people who come from the eastern part of the peninsula). This distinction reflects an essential difference between the culture of the *ahl al-balad* as families in a metropolitan city with a cosmopolitan population, and the culture of the nomadic tribes that have settled around the city but adopted few traits of the city culture.

The fact that the Najdites were not counted among the *ahl al-balad*, and, unlike other ethnic groups, long maintained a separate identity is related to the historical circumstances of their settlement in Jiddah. The earliest Najdite families to immigrate to Jiddah came near the end of Turkish rule. Young men usually arrived without their wives and children. Typically, they started their careers by working in shops owned by older Najdites who had arrived before them and who by then were already set up in business and had their families with them. With the money the young immigrants saved, many opened stores of their own and gradually expanded their trade to include the export business. After achieving some security, they would bring their wives to Jiddah. Although Najdites began immigrating by the end of the Turkish period, it was only by the time of the Ashraf that they had become enterpreneurs and had ceased to be the owners of humble grocery stores. This was also the time when Ibn Sa'ud threatened the supremacy of the Ashraf over the Hijaz. Being of the same ethnic group as Ibn Sa'ud, the Najdites were politically disadvantaged and regarded with suspicion. Although there is no published record of this period, interviews with old Najdites suggest that this situation hindered and delayed assimilation into the dominant *ahl al-balad* culture. For example, gathering of men in a Najdite house seldom included *ahl al-balad*.

When Ibn Sa'ud conquered Jiddah and ended Ashraf rule by establishing himself as King of the Hijaz in 1926 with Jiddah as the temporary seat of government, the position of the Najdites changed. Then, their ethnicity worked to their advantage, and they sought to maintain their identity as Najdites and enjoy the opportunities that it provided. Not surprisingly, then, no marriage between Najdites and elite *ahl al-balad* had occurred before the Ibn Sa'ud period.

Gradually, after the outset of the king's rule, it became an increasing practice for Najdites to marry with members of the *ahl al-balad* families. The offspring from these unions, being partly Najdites and partly *ahl al-balad*, have been in a position to stress that cultural strand of their background which they felt would stand them in better stead, depending on the circumstances. In the main the Najdites have adopted an *ahl al-balad* way of life, although I have reason to believe that some distinctions are still made and matter for career civil servants. However, these distinctions do not seem to be evident in the domestic setting. Since neither marriage arrangements nor patterns of social interaction among women indicate such distinctions, they appear to be irrelevant to the aims of this study.

The description and analysis in this book will focus on the changing trends in ideology—here defined as the set of norms and ideals which people employ to organize their lives and act with some measure of predictability to achieve their purposes—and in social organization of the elite segment of the *ahl al-balad* population. Neither these changing trends nor their elite status detract from their membership in this population. However, their status with its behavioral correlates does serve as a source for introducing changes in the ideology and culture patterns of the wider community.

The People

My research involved thirteen families belonging to three generations which I have delineated by crucial historical events. The oldest generation includes people between the ages of fifty and eighty whose first children were born after Ibn Sa'ud unified the part of the peninsula that now constitutes the Kingdom of Saudi Arabia. The middle generation comprises those people whose first children were born during and after the Second World War. And the younger generation is made up of those postwar children who have reached marriage age over the past two decades.

The term "family" (*'a'ilah*) as used in this study denotes a group of people who share common agnatic descent, that is, belong to the same patrilineage. The term *ahl* refers to an unbounded bilateral group that contains ego's parents; parents' parents and their siblings; siblings and their children; siblings' children's children; children; children's children, plus all of ego's agnates not included among these. The inclusion of other matrilineal consanguinal relatives depends upon their frequency of social interaction with ego's natal family. The term *arham* refers to relatives married into ego's *ahl* or ego's spouse's *ahl*.

While a woman, upon marriage, becomes incorporated in the household of her husband, she remains a member of her natal family. As I shall explain in chapter 2, the composition of a household varies considerably, and the different patterns of coresidence do not warrant a simple definition. It is, therefore, easier to consider the number of families studied to determine how well my data portray the culture of the Jiddah elite. Since no informant listed more than thirty families of elite status, the thirteen families with which I was able to work represent 43 percent of the total number of elite families in the city. This estimate is supported by the fact that a

Table
Dimensions of Elite Status Weighted By Generation

Dimensions of Elite Status	GENERATION		
(= Prestige)	I	II	III
Reputation (R)	R_1	R_1	R_1
Descent (D)	D_1	D_2	D_3
Piety (P)	P_1	P_2	P_3
Wealth (W)	W_3	W_2	W_1
Individual Achievement (A)	A_3	A_2	A_1

Subscripts indicate relative importance of dimensions for different generations, where $1 > 2 > 3$.

local historian has included all but two of the families of my sample in his list of forty prominent Jiddah families.[11]

While the group of families studied included three Najdite families, their common elite status and its behavioral correlates in Jiddah society make their regional origin little more than a biographical note. In fact, their elite status distinguishes all these families from other *ahl al-balad*, whatever their ethnicity may be. This status results from a combination of the following dimensions of prestige: reputation, descent, piety, wealth, and individual achievement.

The concept of prestige subsumes a cluster of features that together signify its evaluative meaning. The attributed strength of these variables to a family constitutes its prestige. The table shows the differences in relative importance of the five dimensions of prestige over the three generations.

The first dimension of prestige is *reputation*. This refers essentially to moral behavior of men and women. For the women this means that they veil in public, that they do not gamble or drink alcohol, and that they maintain decorous distance in their interaction with men. Specifically, older-generation women I studied rarely left the home. When they did, they covered their face and hair in public. They met unveiled only men whom they could not marry, something that obtained even inside the house. The women in the middle and younger generations have a modified view of the veil's importance. They agree that covering the face should be observed in the traditional marketplace and in the downtown area. Elsewhere, if the face is not veiled, it should be free of makeup and other forms of beautification, because an unveiled, beautified face is considered seductive to men—a matter which threatens the family's honor and bears negatively on its reputation. Excessive exposure of the body, as in a minidress or a low-cut neckline, is also inappropriate for women. Even in women's gatherings, such attire "shocks" people, one younger-generation woman explained, and "this affects the reputation of the girl's family."

Not all the middle and younger generation considered the presence of married women in mixed gatherings to be damaging to the reputation of their families. In fact, they approved of such gatherings, provided that they were held in a domestic setting, were attended by married couples, and that women strictly observed appropriate social distance from men. Physical contact between the sexes, except for formal handshaking upon entry and departure, and jokes with sexual connotations were viewed as inappropriate familiarity with men. People reject the presence of unmarried women in such gatherings "because others might say the family is exhibiting its women to the men in order to secure husbands for them." Drinking alcohol and gambling violate strict tabus for women in all three generations. Infractions of these tabus entail a scandalous blow to the reputation of the woman's family, whether she is single or married.

Although the reputation of a family is also affected by the conduct of its male members, their violation of social norms regarding gambling and drinking, indiscretion in their association with women, and even business dealings is less harmful. Older-generation members regarded drinking as a tabu that must be observed by men in private and in public. But middle and younger generations have a modified view which condemns only excessive drinking, especially in public, as adversely affecting a family's reputation. Affairs with women (who are never Saudis, but usually European, Egyptian, Syrian, or Lebanese), although not encouraged, are permitted for men before and after marriage, provided that they are

discreet and out of the public eye. It is only when a man's relations
with women become public knowledge that they are felt to reflect
badly on his family's reputation. Similarly, while honesty in business dealings is a virtue, a measure of clever maneuvering in favor
of one's interests is tolerated, as long as it involves no public
scandal.

Amity among relatives—*ahl* and *arham* alike—represents another
aspect of the reputation dimension of elite status. Mutual visiting
of kinsmen enhances a family's reputation. The frequency of such
visits is not as important as their timing for occasions related to the
life cycle (birth, naming, marriage, and death), as well as for religiously important occasions, such as the feast ending Ramadan
and the feast of the pilgrimage. Financial help by the wealthier men
to poor kinsmen and to women without male supporters among *ahl*
and *arham* also increases a family's "good reputation." On the other
hand, intrafamily conflict, especially when known to the community, injuries its reputation.

Descent refers to a person's ancestry. For the indigenous population good descent means to belong to the Sadah or Ashraf, who
claim the Prophet as their agnatic ancestor. For the Najdites good
descent means to belong to the Shuyukh, who claim descent from
"strong, powerful" tribes and whose ancestors have not engaged in
unprestigious professions. However, good descent is usually defined by the absence of certain categories of people from one's
patrilineage: slaves, *mawalid* (offspring of marriages between slave
and nonslave), *takruni* (Africans), or Yemenis. The importance of
this dimension in determining elite status, while still present, has
declined over the three generations. The younger generation feels
that individual achievement can balance, if not eliminate, the effect
of bad descent on prestige.

Piety refers to the observance of Islamic rituals; a knowledge of
religious doctrine and instruction; *sadaqah*, or almsgiving; donations of the *zakat* tax; building mosques; and other philanthropical
donations. In the older generation individuals consider the practice
of Islamic teachings to include performance of the five daily
prayers, performance of the pilgrimage, and fasting during the
month of Ramadan. The younger-generation members are more
likely to emphasize the public aspects of religious practice, such as
the Friday noon prayer performed in the mosque. But all agree that

a knowledge of the Qu'ran and of liturgical aspects of the religion, and the annual distribution of *zakat* (2½ percent of capital), in addition to almsgiving, constitute important requirements of a pious life.

Wealth implies ownership of residential homes and cars, support of domestic servants, financing children's education, vacation trips abroad, and ownership of real estate, both in Saudi Arabia and abroad. For the older generation, wealth as such did not confer elite status, and other dimensions—especially descent, reputation, and piety—were more important in determining the prestige of a family. For the middle and younger generations, however, wealth facilitated private education and travel, which enhanced the family's prestige. This does not mean that the younger generation views wealth as sufficient to guarantee elite status for a family. Indeed, some wealthy families are considered nonelite for a variety of reasons: either because they are known to have amassed their wealth through devious means; or because they neglected to use their wealth for the schooling of their sons; or because they withheld financial help when poor people sought their aid; or because they denied themselves the luxuries that their wealth made possible, such as vacations overseas, domestic servants, and entertaining. Charity is valued behavior, but the education of sons is a more valued use of wealth. In contrast, some families who cannot afford the life-style of the wealthy still maintain elite status. The history of these families, however, indicates that at least in the preceding generation they had considerable wealth.

Individual achievement comes mainly with schooling and further education, and it is reflected in practicing a profession, managing successful business operations, or holding positions in the higher echelons of administration. These personal qualifications become important with the middle and especially the younger generation. Schooling for males and females in private institutions abroad or now even locally, particularly at the university level, constitutes an asset that makes successful careers possible. But it must be pointed out that, despite the growing acceptance of the education and even employment of women, it is the success of *men* in professional life that enhances a family's prestige. To the younger generation, then, individual achievement and the concomitant social recognition represent determinants of prestige and a means of mobility whereby a physician, for example, with a slave ancestor more remote than his own parents can gain elite status.

For elite families the accumulation of financial resources had other consequences that contributed to the development of a style of life distinct from that of the other *ahl al-balad* people. Early travel abroad (for both men and women) and ownership of property in foreign countries favored this development. The financial means required for journeys abroad were unavailable before the discovery of oil and the economic boom it brought to the country under the present kingdom. During Turkish and Ashraf rule only business-men and agents involved in organizing and supplying pilgrim groups traveled abroad. In that period, women left the country only to obtain medical treatment, especially in Egypt and Syria. As indicated earlier, when Ibn Sa'ud besieged Jiddah, many *ahl al-balad* families who could afford it sent their families to the Sudan, Egypt, India, Ethiopia, or the southern part of the peninsula. They stayed abroad for a number of months and returned only after Ibn Sa'ud came to power. After this period few women traveled abroad until the formation of the kingdom in 1932, and even then their purpose was restricted to medical treatment.

Gradually, as the families became more affluent, these trips in-cluded vacations. Both their financial means and the now frequent trips for men to other Arab countries—mainly Egypt—encouraged investment in real estate, which in turn increased the frequency of trips *en famille*, since a source of income was secured abroad. In fact, this situation allowed the families to take up temporary resi-dence in countries where they owned property. The early years and long exposure of these families to cultural experiences outside Saudi Arabia led to their adoption of values not shared by the rest of the *ahl al-balad*. The women, for example, took on dress and eating habits they saw in Egypt. Although Saudi women continued to veil during their stay in Egypt, they modified the form and use of the veil. The *'aba'*, or floor-length black cloak, was replaced with a coat; and gradually they wore scarves on the head instead of the *tarhah*, the chiffon shawl draped around the face in several layers. Until the 1960s, however, the veil continued to be used in the company of Saudi men met abroad—and even today, a few of the older- and middle-generation women, when abroad, avoid meeting Saudi men whom they could potentially marry.

Another important consequence of their exposure to foreign culture and their temporary residence in different societies was their attitude toward the education of girls. The first girls to enroll in school in the mid-1940s came from families which temporarily lived abroad. In Jiddah at that time there were only informal schools, called *faqihah*s, to tutor girls in reading the Qur'an and in needlework and some arithmetic. They provided education that stopped with puberty, when their strict seclusion at home began and veiling in public became mandatory. Women of the older generation went only to these informal schools, and it was from them that they learned Qur'anic surahs and committed them to memory. Thus, while illiterate, they can "read" the Qur'an.

By the time of the middle generation, some elite families sponsored tutorial groups for girls. Although ideally daughters of all Jiddah families could participate in these groups to learn Arabic, arithmetic, and the Qur'an, in practice they have included only daughters of the elite families. Private tutoring here, as in Macca in the latter part of the nineteenth century, was another means of teaching literacy to women in the middle generation.[12]

Thus, even though some families who had traveled to Egypt by the 1940s wanted to put their daughters in schools, they could do so only if they had temporary residence abroad. Girls were not yet entrusted to boarding schools—a step that was not taken until the early 1950s. Again, the earliest group of girls attending boarding schools in Egypt, and later in Lebanon, came from the elite families.

The initiative for girls' education, whether in informal tutorial groups or in formal schools, often came from their mothers, who, through repeated appeals to their husbands, actualized these possibilities for them. These innovations, along with the partial adoption of Egyptian values, created a distinct life-style that provided incentives for other *ahl al-balad* families, which gradually began to emulate ideas and attitudes held by the elite.

Of all accepted innovations adopted by the elite, one critical change affected the education of girls: when the government started to provide schooling during the 1960s, numerous families readily accepted this opportunity for pursuing new goals that had been validated, as they saw it, by the elite. Similarly, changes initiated by the elite families in marriage and marriage ceremonies, death and condolence ceremonies, dress and eating habits, are increasingly adopted by the rest of the community. Interestingly, their attitudes toward marriage arrangements have changed very little, since elite families themselves have only recently begun to tamper with tradition in this respect. Clearly, the prestige status which is enjoyed by the families studied and which gains them the respect of the community explains why more and more people adopt their life-style. People from nonelite families express their respect for them by seeking their help as intermediaries, in disputes, in securing jobs, in solving problems with the government authorities, and settling family conflicts. Though some of the present heads of household do not act as intermediaries, at one period some individuals in the parental or perhaps grandparental generation did play this role vis-à-vis the rest of the community. Intermediation by the lineage leaders of the families was on the level of the lineage and its *arham* as well as that of the rest of the community. Currently, some lineage "leaders" still intermediate conflicts between lineage members and in the *arham*, but increasingly less so with the rest of the community unless the dispute involves people with whom friendship relations have been maintained.

As the foregoing indicates, the elite has been taking the lead in changing customs and life-styles as well as the ideological underpinnings of their lives. Marx pointed out that those who control the means of production also control mental production, and studies have demonstrated that "hegemonic groups" control the flow of information in a society and edit the world view of others.[13] Similarly, the elite families with which this study is concerned have changed customs and modified ideological beliefs, both of which have spread to the rest of the society.

At this time, it is best to view the relationship between people's practices and their ideologies as coordinate with one another. In other words, statements that practices cause a change in ideology are misleading. Instead, the position taken in this book is that the two reinforce each other. To say as much is to agree that "material *and* ideal interests directly govern men's conduct."[14] This is what the German historian Otto Hintze called the "polar coordination of interests and ideas."[15]

If one takes this view of the nature of the relation between conduct and ideologies, it rapidly becomes clear that people act in the world and, indeed, upon it; but they are themselves also acted upon by this world. In this perspective, as Giddens has put it: "Reality is not merely 'external' to man, shaping his consciousness, but is adapted to human ends through the active application of consciousness and the modification of the pre-existing environment."[16]

Otherwise put, if a particular group adopts a specific set of beliefs as a guide to action, this does not mean that the consequences of their behavior are a direct result of the influence of those beliefs. In the same way, the kind of existence led by a particular group may induce them to adopt certain beliefs, but this does not necessarily mean that their form of existence determines the content of such beliefs. Thus, urban merchants, who presumably employ a rational calculus, means/ends perspective in their business, might opt for a religious ideology that stresses extreme frugality and abstinence. But it would be foolish to argue that only urban entrepreneurs can or do opt for ascetic religious commitment.[17]

This essential point about the "polar coordination" of domestic group practices and ideology will appear forcefully in the central chapters of this book. Unidirectional causality is thus avoided to bring out a more complex interrelationship between practices and ideology.

A second analytical point will be stressed here. This study argues that as one looks at the three generations of women, a general trend of movement away from the extended family to the nuclear family is at work. As will be seen, this tendency is making a significant impact on a wide range of issues affecting these women's lives. This can be seen most immediately at the level of postnuptial residential patterns, since the way people live is a visible indication of how they arrange their relationships. A gradual shift has taken place from viripatrilocal to semineolocal to neolocal residence. As separate entrances and exits are established in the home, contact between married couples and their parents tends to be reduced. Preferences for the newer forms of residential patterns are a consequence of newly acquired values by both men and women of the younger generation.

The above process of movement from extended to nuclear family can also be captured in the growing tendency of women to cut down on the webs of relationships that traditionally have linked them in rather wide-ranging networks of friends and relatives. The newer pattern appears to be more time spent between husband and wife, more involvement of women in decisions affecting their children and their immediate family, in monitoring of the household activities, and in control of the family budget. Physical distance from the parental generation has translated for the younger-generation wife into relative autonomy from her mother-in-law; and for the younger-generation man, into relative if not great independence from his father.

In their neolocal homes women's conjugal roles have become less segregated as their duties have come to include the supervision, upbringing, and education of both daughters *and* sons. Wifely duties that were always important even for the older generation now have come to take precedence over friendship duties—a matter that was not problematical for the older generation. Evident, therefore, in the Jiddah case is that when women were more secluded, they sought to widen their social world through creating and sustaining friendship networks that played an important role in their lives. Such networks gave them information about the society at large and a source of financial and emotional support.

As younger-generation women became less secluded, as their conjugal roles became less segregated, and as they gained more autonomy from the extended family, they spent less time and effort in their friendship networks, especially when these involved friends of their parents. What is happening here is a gradual substitution of one set of relationships (conjugal) for another (friendship).

The data show that the realms of security and insecurity are changing for the women who are the subject of this study. There is no question but that the structural asymmetry between men and women in Jiddah remains stable, but particularly noteworthy is that increasing discretion is available for women who want to make use of it. The changing domains of discretion and constraint are, then, in large measure what this book is about.

Perhaps this can be shown more clearly by the following considerations on seclusion and power asymmetry. Several writers have speculated about the "reason" for the seclusion of women and their restricted participation in extrahousehold affairs in the Middle East and in India, where the Hindu and Muslim institution of purdah enforces these norms.[18] Most ethnographies dealing with this problem describe considerable variations in the degree to which people in the same society who belong to different economic levels practice the ideal of maintaining spatial and visual barriers between the sexes. These observed intrasocietal differences provide clues to the development and distribution of the custom. In answer to the question of when societies can afford to institute a rigid segregation of the sexes, I have proposed and still maintain that women's seclusion varies, inter alia, with the extent to which they participate in the economy.[19] Specifically, the greater the women's contribution to the subsistence economy from work done outside the house (gardening, gathering, farming, or herding), the greater will be their freedom of movement and participation in public life. Conversely, the less women contribute to the subsistence economy from work done outside the house, the more restricted will be their freedom of movement and participation in public life.

Among Middle Eastern peasants, as well as other peasants (for example, India),[20] the demand for female labor outside the house lessens the restrictions on women's mobility that wealthier families, able to hire help, can afford to enforce. Thus, Barclay reports for a Sudanese village that "with the increase in wealth and access to modern facilities, more women may be expected to remain within the compound, whereas the greater the poverty, the less the seclusion of women."[21] Similar conditions reduce the confinement of women to the house in the towns and villages of Iran and Palestine.[22] These observations attach yet another value to the concealment of women. It serves as a status marker, symbolizing the socioeconomic rank that facilitates its enforcement.[23]

Although sexual separateness may sometimes be congruent with models of complementarity and equality between the sexes, the evidence of this study correlates strict segregation with male dominance, on both the ideological and the behavioral levels.[24] Recent theoretical studies in anthropology, especially by feminist scholars, have offered sophisticated theories to understand and explain such power asymmetry.[25] Some explanations stress economic factors, while others give more importance to cultural features. From the point of view of this book a fuller explanation of power asymmetry has to be sought in cultural ideological as well as economic and political factors, which, in their totality, affect the distribution of power between the sexes.[26]

For *ahl al-balad* elite families relative economic affluence is one of the traditional criteria determining their status in the community. Such affluence, of course, differentiates these women from nonelite women. One may agree with Friedl, who, in another context, suggests that these women's higher social rank sometimes overrides their sexual ranking.[27] In the Jiddah case, relative to men of lower status, these women have power and are given deference; they are sought as intermediaries for men and women to get jobs, loans, etc. Their power is different from that of men because these attributes are not legitimately recognized as the right of women and remain a consequence of their personalities and the status of their husbands and fathers.

However, vis-à-vis men in their own families (and ignoring age differences) these women's means have not translated into less asymmetry of power between men and women. Their wealth has remained squarely under the control of men; although women have the right to own property, they rarely manage it themselves. So, effectively and until recent years women have had neither control of property nor control of income that would guarantee their economic autonomy from husbands or male agnates.[28]

As for political factors, it is clear that men control political decisions affecting the community at large; yet, women also have political power, expressed in their de facto control of domestic life, in addition to marriages that extend beyond the "private domain" of the women's world. While men's control of the polity is, of course, control of crucial institutions in the society, so is women's active participation in arranging marriages (and control of certain stages of marriage negotiations) which have important economic and political implications for the society at large. For this reason, in the case of Jiddah domestic elites, the private/public distinction sometimes used to understand gender asymmetry is not useful.[29] The contrast between the "domestic" and the outside world is not relevant to marriages that result in a network of ties combining economic, political, and social implications for men and women alike. When we look at these kinship implications, for example, and at the network of exchange between men and women (as in the social visits discussed in chapter 4) the view of women in elite Jiddah families changes to one where their status in the society as a whole finds cultural compensation in a network of friendship through which women forge and maintain ties of support and emotional succor. These same networks avail them information about community events and especially make the selection of marriage partners for their sons possible. Their control of such information is critical to their marriage strategies, which see women engaged in enhancing their autonomy within the wider limits of family interests.

For the younger generation of women, a new domain of control is emerging. This is the domain of property rights, which women are asserting with growing frequency. It is likely that this development indicates a shift that is still in process and by no means completed. Moreover, as will be clear later in the analysis, the areas of male control subsume those of women's control. This minimizes women's power and gives men more prestige, resulting in unequal power for men and women.[30]

NOTES

1. Soraya Altorki, "The Anthropologist in the Field."
2. Abd al-Quddus Al-Ansari, *Ta'rikh Madinat Jiddah,* p. 52.
3. Ayishah bint 'Abdullah Baqasi, *Bilad al-Hijaz fi al-'Asr al-Ayyubi,* p. 63.
4. *Ibid.,* pp. 63 ff.
5. Ahmad Siba'i, *Ta'rikh Macca,* 1:197, 225. Pilgrims who came from Syria or via Syria at that time proceeded to Egypt and thence took the same route to the Hijaz. Later, they met the pilgrimage route at 'Aqabah.
6. Ahmad Siba'i, *Ta'rikh Macca,* 2:104.
7. *Ibid.,* 2:269. the Ashraf (singular, Sharif) local ruling families who claim the Prophet, Muhammad, as agnatic ancestor. They had ruled Macca since 'Abbasid times. Their rule was punctuated by rivalries among their different factions, and by allegiance—whether nominal or real—to the Mamluks of Egypt, Muhammad 'Ali's dynasty in Egypt, and Ottoman Turkey. Effective and formal control of Jiddah by the Ashraf came in 1916, when Sharif Husayn, backed by the British, proclaimed Arab independence and captured Jiddah from the Turkish representative, declaring it the capital of the Hijaz. In 1925, after almost a year's siege, the city fell to Ibn Sa'ud, who ousted the Ashraf and established the current dynasty.
8. *Ibid.,* 2:250. The party was dissolved in 1924.

9. *Ibid.*, 2:101.

10. Al-Ansari, *Ta'rikh Madinat Jiddah*, p. 153.

11. *Ibid.*, pp. 281 ff.

12. Snouck Hurgronje, *Mekka*, p. 115.

13. Nels Johnson, *Islam and the Politics of Meaning in Palestinian Nationalism*.

14. Reinhard Bendix, *Max Weber*, p. 46, citing Weber.

15. *Ibid.*, p. 47.

16. Anthony Giddens, *Capitalism and Modern Social Theory*, p. 210.

17. *Ibid.*, p. 211.

18. See, for example, Nur Yalman, "On the Purity of Women in the Castes of Ceylon and Malaber"; Richard Antoun, "On the Modesty of Women in Arab Muslim Villages"; Emrys Peters, "Aspects of Rank and Status Among Muslims in a Lebanese Village"; and Doranne Jacobson, "Hidden Faces."

19. Soraya Altorki, "Religion and Social Organization of Elite Families in Urban Saudi Arabia."

20. See Gerald Berreman, *Hindus of the Himalayas*.

21. Harold B. Barclay, *Burri al-Lamaab*, p. 13.

22. See Paul Ward English, *City and Village in Iran*, and Abner Cohen, *Arab Border Villages in Israel*, for conditions in Iran and Palestine, respectively.

23. Papanek makes the same point about purdah in India and Pakistan and adds further that seclusion is associated with men's control over women, and a view of purdah as "symbolic shelter" from the world outside the house, which is perceived to be hostile to women. Hanna Papanek, "Purdah."

24. However, on the basis of what we now know, it is evident that such dominance cannot be posited a priori, as research has revealed greater cultural diversity than previously assumed. The distribution of power between men and women in society was for long obscured partly by an androcentric bias in anthropology and sometimes by an ethnocentric bias that saw other societies in terms of cultural givens of Western society. For a critique of these views, see Rayner Rapp, "Review Essay: Anthropology"; Jane Monning Atkinson, "Review Essay: Anthropology"; and Sylvia Junko Yanagisaro, "Family and Household." Another reason was the traditional preoccupation with formal structures of power (in the polity) to the exclusion of informal expressions of power. See Susan Carol Rogers, "Female Forms of Power and the Myth of Male Dominance," and Soraya Altorki, "Family Organization and Women's Power in Urban Saudi Arabian Society."

25. Generally speaking, some have assumed that such asymmetry is universal. See, for example, Sherry B. Ortner, "Is Female to Male as Nature is to Culture?"; Jane Fishburne Collier and Michelle Zimbalist Rosaldo, "Politics and Gender in Simple Societies"; Rosaldo, "Women, Culture, and Society: A Theoretical Overview"; and Rosaldo, "The Use and Abuse of

Anthropology." The reasons for such universality are women's child bearing role, their relegation to the domestic, unvalued domain, and their association with nature versus men's association with culture. See, respectively, N. Chodorow, "Family Structure and Feminine Personality"; Rosaldo, "Women, Culture, and Society"; and Ortner "Is Female to Male?"

Others, especially Marxists, have argued that asymmetry is the result of specific historical conditions related to relations of distribution, to the rise of private ownership and the emergence of classes, the transformation of relations of production and the emergence of the state. See, respectively, Ernestine Friedl, *Women and Men;* Eleanor Burke Leacock, "Introduction to Frederick Engels" ; Karen Sacks, "Engels Revisited"; Mina Davis Caufield, "Equality, Sex, and the Mode of Production"; and June Nash, "The Aztecs and the Ideology of Male Dominance."

Still others posit that sexual asymmetry is a consequence of private property as well as of policies of kinship and marriage; that ideology as well as productive and social relations affects sexual stratification; and the sex role plans (i.e., cultural ideological factors), in addition to environmental and historical ones, lead to male dominance. For these views see, respectively, Gayle Rubin, "The Traffic in Women"; Collier and Rosaldo, "Politics and Gender in Simple Societies"; Alice Schlegel, ed. *Sexual Stratification;* and Peggy Sanday, *Female Power and Male Dominance.*

26. See Schlegel, *Sexual Stratification;* Sanday, *Female Power and Male Dominance.* In this book "power" is defined as an individual's ability to influence the behavior of others.

27. See Friedl, *Women and Men.*

28. I have suggested elsewhere that control of property is as important as rights to property in assessing the distribution and control of resources between men and women in the society. See Altorki, "Religion and Social Organization."

29. The private/public dichotomy is potentially misleading. The distinction between private and public domains as a tool for understanding gender asymmetry has not been supported by empirical research in societies where such distinctions skewed the far-reaching implications of kinship, women exchange networks, and the political dimensions of women's activities. See Rapp, "Review Essay"; Schlegel, *Sexual Stratification;* Sanday, *Female Power and Male Dominance;* Atkinson, "Review Essay"; Yanagisaro, "Family and Household."

30. See Ortner and Whitehead, eds., *Sexual Meanings.*

CHAPTER TWO

HOME AND HOUSEHOLD

THIRTY TO FORTY years ago the families I studied lived in what is today the downtown area of Jiddah. It was then also the area where they conducted their businesses, which primarily involved wholesale and retail marketing of imported food, especially rice, tea, and sugar. Some men held government posts, usually as higher-level administrators; but invariably, they supplemented their salaries with trading. Others were pilgrimage agents, who drew their income from housing pilgrims in Jiddah, Macca, and Madina and from arranging their transport and supplying the paraphernalia needed for the performance of the *hajj*.[1] The absence of hotels made such an agency a lucrative business, particularly when it served pilgrims known to be wealthy: Indonesians and Persians, for example. Like any other business, these agencies were competitive ventures. Agents competed in recruiting pilgrims through representatives stationed in foreign countries—and luring pilgrims away from other agents even after their arrival in Jiddah.

Being relatively wealthy, these merchant families were the first to purchase land beyond the city wall, where they built new homes when the downtown area became crowded. Their villas now cluster along two main roads: Madina Road, which links Jiddah to the city of Madina in the north, and Macca Road, connecting to Macca in the east. At the beginning these areas were inhabited predominantly by the wealthy elite, but since the late 1960s people from different economic strata moved there when houses and apartments became available for rent. In the mid-1970s, many of the elite families moved still further away from the old boundaries of the city as its commercial center expanded toward the north and south. Today, the Madina and Macca roads neighborhoods have become quite heterogeneous both in class and in ethnic composition.

Whereas buildings in the old section of the city were constructed with limestone (which is abundant in the area), the houses built during the past 25 to 30 years are made of cement and conform to a Western style of architecture. All *ahl al-balad* elite families now live in two- or three-storey villas, set in gardens that are surrounded by a three- to four-meter-high fence. The older homes are enclosed by higher fences, which, along with partial brick cover on the balconies, shield the women from the sight of passersby and neighbors.

The interiors of the villas vary in luxury and in the mixture of Arab and Western styles, the latter being the more prominent the newer the home. In general, the use of armchairs in salons, dining tables and chairs, beds, air conditioners, refrigerators, gas ovens, washing machines, prints or paintings, radio, television and video cassette recorders, record players, and tape recorders reflects both an adoption of Western aesthetic values and a dependence on imported appliances for the families' domestic comfort. Where the traditional style has been preserved, it is reflected in the simple furnishings of the salon, or living room, with Persian carpets and a series of cotton mattresses with backrests and pillows placed in the sitting areas along the walls. The women did and still do spend much of their time in this room; and formerly, an elaborate tea-making apparatus was set up in its corner. All meals used to be served in this room, on a tablecloth spread on the floor. While a few of the elite families continue the tradition of serving food on common plates from which all present may still eat by hand, most of them now have complete dining rooms, although their use is limited to the main meal.

A typical old house includes a wing for the men, usually on the first floor, with an access to the garden and to the ground-floor balconies. In this part of the house the head of the household has his sleeping room, study, guest rooms, and sitting rooms. The second and third floors belong to the women: one for daily living and another for receiving guests. The pattern varies if married men live in their parents' house. In this case the first floor, with separate wings for men and women, usually belongs to the parents, and the third floor belongs to the eldest son, as it is considered the best part of the house and would be occupied by the parents if they did not mind climbing stairs. The second-eldest married son has his living quarters on the second floor.

The traditional pattern of allocating space facilitated a strict segregation of men and women, and its recent change reflects a modification of this segregation. The older generation maintained separate floors for men and women, each containing special rooms where guests were received and entertained. Husband and wife seldom shared the same sleeping quarters, the husband's bedroom sometimes being on a different floor. Children of both sexes slept with their mother or nanny, but "once their bodies developed," i.e., between seven and nine years, boys and girls were placed apart at different ends of the room with the mother or nanny in the middle. When the boys reached puberty, they moved to the men's quarter of the house.

The middle and younger generations, if they have a separate house, no longer observe these rules. Their homes have no separate quarters. Guests of both sexes are either entertained in the same room at different times or received jointly if such practice is tolerated by the head of the household. In such settings, husband and wife share a bedroom, which may have an annex for their youngest children (until these are seven or eight years old). The eldest children of both sexes share another room until reaching puberty.

Male and female servants occupy different sleeping quarters in the houses of all three generations. The men's quarters are outside the house but always within the garden fence, and the women have a separate room in the house. During the day, younger male servants who do the cleaning move freely through the women's quarters, and even older men, if they are cooks, drivers, or gardeners, enter the house when called. However, older informants insisted that this situation developed within the last ten to fifteen years "as people made a habit of traveling and began to imitate the people abroad." Before, houseboys were barred from the female quarters, and on reaching puberty they were assigned to the garden or to an office.

The predominant pattern of residence for the older generation was viripatrilocal, i.e., a woman moved to her husband's father's house, where she had a room, an apartment on a floor, or a whole floor to herself, depending on the size of the house. This arrangement was advantageous insofar as sons usually joined their father's business. The father continued to provide the budget for the whole household, unless a son's independent business ventures made him richer than his father, in which case he contributed to the budget with a monthly sum for food and/or by paying for his own servants. As opportunities for trade and marketing expanded and men of the middle generation acquired far greater wealth than their fathers had, they also began to assume full financial responsibility for the joint household.

The unity of the traditional patrilocal household was also reflected in the *wu'ud*, an institution of formal social visits between women. Even when guests were not common friends of all coresident women, a formal visit always involved them all, and the unexplained absence of anyone expected to be present indicated strained relations among the women in the household. Formal friends (*wufyan*) were generally received either in the salon of the mother or in the quarters of her new daughter-in-law (so that the guests could see her trousseau). The desire to present collective amity was so strong that the women coordinated the visits of their *wufyan*, so that everyone would be present on the day of the visit.

The middle generation by and large continued these residence arrangements. In the few cases where a man decided to establish his own residence, he had returned to Jiddah after having lived with his wife in another city for a time. The financial responsibility for the joint household, where it persists, has also remained unchanged. Where sons work for their father, the latter provides for the household budget, but where sons have an independent business they contribute to the budget with their own and their father's means. If the father is considerably wealthier than the son, he still provides for his son's family, including the schooling of his children both in Jiddah and abroad. For the younger generation residence arrangements have become much more flexible, and patterns are not easily detected except that the trend toward neolocal residence has become more pronounced, whether or not the son is working in his father's business and whether or not he still depends on paternal help to support his own independent household. When young men decide to live patrilocally, they prefer to live in a separate villa in the compound of the parental house, as well as maintain separate eating arrangements, even if the two households support a common kitchen.

The shift to neolocal residence is related to differences in experience, education, and values that exist between the men of the older and younger generations. Such a shift, which is relatively recent, has implications for holding mixed social gatherings. Establishing residential distance between parents and sons, neolocal residence allows each generation to follow its own customs while reducing the conflict that changes entail. Traditional tabus against holding mixed social gatherings are breaking down, therefore, and in Jiddah more than in Riyadh. Usually, such gatherings bring together married couples who are *ahl, arham,* or friends. The implicit guidelines for participation are sharing the same attitudes and allowing one's wife to be present.

This development was hardly foreseeable by the parents who built huge houses to accommodate separate wings for married sons, most of which now stand empty. As one old man (who himself maintains a patrilocal compound) explained: "These days, young people want to live their lives their own way, which is different from ours. Unless one can provide them with this privacy, they'll leave [the father's house]. I have my married son live with me because I do not interfere in his family's life. Each can come and go as he pleases and do whatever he likes in his house." This compound has separate entrances for the sons still living in their father's house and a separate villa for the eldest son.

Neolocal residence also reflects a desire of wives in the younger generation to assert their autonomy vis-à-vis their husbands' mothers. As an old woman (who lives with her son's wife) said: "When young girls get married, they make it a condition to live alone. When a man goes to ask for a girl's hand in marriage, the family asks, 'Where will she live?' A girl wants to move out because she wants to feel that she is the mistress of her new home. They want the liberty to go and come without notifying their mothers-in-law, which they would have to do if they lived in the same house. Now sons move out if they can afford it. If not, then their fathers help them build a house. Anyway, too close a contact between a man's mother and his wife brings misunderstandings. In the past the husband's mother was the mistress of the house. Now the young girl wants this position for herself. When a son gets married, his mother is jealous of the attention he gives his wife, and she is angry because he can no longer spend so much time with her as he did before his marriage. So, after all, distance between the woman and her daughter-in-law is a good thing."

The norms of residence set the wider limits of expected behavior in the society. Within these limits individuals make choices in accordance with their economic, social, and cultural interests. Such interests are, of course, circumscribed in the end by their specific interpretation of the dominant ideology in their society. Consequently, we find variations in these residence patterns that become clearer as we move from the middle to the younger generation. Such variations are not idiosyncratic or haphazard. Their regularity is best understood in terms of the overall changes in Saudi Arabia, which have resulted in a reformulation of the older values and norms.

Throughout and over the three generations postmarital residence, in its gradual change from viripatrilocal to neolocal, results from economic realities (as, for example, a son's greater wealth than his father's); and also from the currency of new values of relative independence from parental authority for the married couple. For the married man of the middle, and especially the younger, generation neolocal residence means an opportunity to establish his own household where he is de facto head. For the middle- and especially younger-generation woman, it means attaining autonomy from her husband's mother's control and an opportunity to live her life according to the values that her education and greater contact with the outside world have made possible for her. These changes in residence patterns have been gradual and, in fact, reflect the interrelationship between norm observances, on the one hand, and on the other the strategies of individuals to redefine these norms.

Especially noticeable in "new homes" is less spatial segregation of men and women as the same space is used by both sexes or by each at a different time. The trend toward integrated residential space relates also to male-female relations within the household. While the spatial arrangements of the older generation separated the "world of women" from the "world of men," it gave each an autonomy from the other. Thus, women escaped the close supervision of men and gained relative autonomy from them in their quarters. Since husband and wife had few joint activities (as we shall see in chapter 3), such spatial segregation was no obstacle to the daily routine in the household.

With the middle- and especially the younger-generation couples, mixed spatial living patterns are perceived as more convenient and in line with the modified views of the norms governing (1) segregation of women and (2) conjugal relationships. In addition, spatial segregation becomes increasingly expensive, even for the elite, as facilities have to be duplicated without "a good reason," as a younger-generation man put it. Husband and wife in these generations—and especially the younger—spend more time together and engage in more joint decisions. The spatial desegregation of their residences reflects the modifications they have brought to the norms of conjugal relations followed by the older generation.

The changes in the extent of women's residential segregation that have occurred over three generations are markedly reflected in the use of the veil. Wearing the veil was, and still is, a conspicuous part of men-women relations in Saudi society. However, as these relations have changed, the practice of veiling has been modified as well.

When asked why women should veil, male and female informants usually reply that "our religion says so." The veil functions as a portable shield which protects women from being seen by any potential husband. But further probing reveals reasons similar to those described by Mernissi in terms of what she calls the "explicit theory" of sexual interaction in Islamic culture.[2] According to this theory, men are sexually aggressive and require that women veil themselves lest the men be roused to *fitnah*, disorderly behavior. Interestingly, the term also means *femme fatale*, a woman who can drive men to distraction and destruction. Implied in such a theory is the notion that it is women who are the aggressive agents, with the further implication that men are too weak to stand their ground against unveiled women; and further, that if men are to be encouraged to continue in their rightful social and religious conduct, then male domination has to be secured through an institutional structure of sexual segregation.[3]

The notion that both men and women are sexually aggressive is reiterated by Hildred Geertz. Among Moroccans in her study, she notes, sexuality is considered to be a quality endowed in men and women by Allah. Thus it is not something which can somehow be preempted or regulated. Such regulation is achieved by reference to Islamic law, *shari'ah*, and community enforcement. The *shari'ah*, notes Geertz, extends its protective provisions to the family, the stability of which it considers to be of paramount importance. The veil thus becomes a means of maintaining the family against threats of disintegration, for it forces both men and women to maintain social distance from one another.[4]

If the veil is meant to prevent any male who is a woman's potential husband from looking upon her, the only persons for whom a woman need not veil are her grandfathers, her father, her brothers, her sons, her grandsons, and those men who could not marry her by virtue of an existing affinal link. The customary preference for marrying the child of a paternal uncle further reduces the already minimal contact between cousins who, in the traditional, patrilocal extended family, used to grow up in the same household. In this regard, research has shown in another context that children who are brought up together in free association tend to seek their spouses from outside their domestic group.[5] If this sociogenic barrier to marriage applies cross-culturally, the veil could be regarded as a device to obviate the negative effect of joint residence on preferred marriage arrangements in Arab society. In short, far from being the "exotic" or "odd" vestige of a "quaint" tradition, veiling may in fact be seen as functional for the maintenance of patrilateral cousin marriage patterns.

In Jiddah girls begin to wear the veil before they reach full puberty, but veiling becomes mandatory with the onset of menstruation. The veil consists of two parts: a black cloak, worn over the dress, which falls from the shoulders down to the ground, and a one-and-one-half to two-meter long chiffon shawl that is draped around the head, covering the face in several layers. The *'ulama'* have cited Qur'anic verse (Q. 33:59) and sayings of the Prophet *(ahadith)* to justify the observance of veiling as a religious duty. However, in the early 1970s they came out with a less stringent view. Women are now permitted to bare their faces and hands when they are on their pilgrimage and during prayer in a mosque.

Much earlier, popular practice among the *ahl al-balad* elite families had already changed the custom at home. Initially, the old women left their faces bare, but changes more radical than this were introduced by women of the middle generation who had traveled and lived abroad for long periods of time. These women were able to modify veiling practices while abroad, although the entire matter was contingent upon their husbands' wishes. The married daughters of these middle-generation women are even more lax in the use of the veil. Of course, unmarried younger-generation women present a different story; stricter observance is the rule, owing to their fathers' views and to the importance of keeping "proper" standards of behavior for the purpose of later finding a husband. Thus from a full-length veil worn by the older-generation women, the garment has become a shorter cloak—black or dark blue in color—that ends just below the knee. It is usually worn over a full-length dress or loosely fitting trousers but sometimes even over a medium-length dress.

Ultimately, whatever the changes that have become widely acceptable, the standards find their justification in, and are sanctioned by, an Islamic doctrine that popular social values have modified in practice. Thus, while all people still acknowledge the omission of the veiling to be *dhanb* (i.e., sinful in the strictly orthodox sense), and even *harām* (tabu, absolutely forbidden), women in the middle and especially the younger generations fear divine retribution less than the social stigma that attaches to shameless behavior. Whether leaving one's hair uncovered or wearing fashionable dress invites stigmatization depends upon the social contexts in which a woman ignores the tabu. The limits to which a woman can "expose" herself are culturally negotiable. To show up in the marketplace without a hair scarf is still considered a sin by unrelenting traditionalists, and a shameless act by all. To appear at a mixed gathering of "close friends" in an *haute couture* dress of "decent" cut is acceptable by those whose very presence at the gathering indicates their liberal view in such matters, although that view does not extend beyond the confines of the shared privacy which the occasion provides.

Historically, veiling practices changed in consequence of foreign travel, which did not begin for women before the early 1930s. While living with their families in Egypt, for example, the men would allow their wives and daughters to wear a coat instead of the cloak and to leave their faces uncovered, unless they were in the company of other men from Saudi Arabia. With time the clothing code adopted abroad became less and less stringent, and by the mid-1950s women of the middle generation appeared in jackets or cardigans worn over sleeveless dresses. By then even the presence of Saudi men no longer demanded the use of the veil, although older women, to this day, have continued to cover their hair, and until a few years ago even some women of the middle generation would not appear when their husbands' friends came for a visit. The women who now belong to the younger generation have never used the veil in any of its forms when they were outside their country. But even they make sure to carry one along to be donned as their plane approaches Jiddah airport.

Other local circumstances, too, have permitted a general relaxation of the veiling custom. Neolocal residence itself isolates women from potential husbands at home, and the exclusive use of private cars, even for going a very short distance, reduces their visibility outside. Still, in the shopping areas cloak and hair scarf are always worn by women of all ages, but generally only the unmarried are obliged to wear the facial veil. Within the last five years or so even that has changed, so that veiling the face may be observed in the traditional market area but is seldom done in the many Western-style shopping centers that have opened in the new areas of the city.

At home, as I have explained, spatial segregation alone has largely controlled men's visual access to the women of the household. Only men who are no longer potential husbands are received by the women, and only those "close friends" with whom ties of mutual trust and confidence have long been established are permitted to enter a room where men and women of the household sit together. Consequently, women now discard the veil completely in the presence of many people, including domestic servants, both *ahl* and *arham* relatives, physicians, and long-time friends. However, an older woman still appears veiled in the presence of a man of her own age group unless he is a relative toward whom she never veiled—her husband's brother or sister's husband, for example.

Married women of the middle generation veil themselves neither to married kinsmen nor to *arham* even if they belong to the same age group, but they wear the veil in the presence of others, such as their husbands' friends, even if they have met these men "openly" abroad. The unmarried, regardless of their age, still do not appear unveiled except to close relatives who are considerably younger; they veil themselves to older men and men of their own generation—married and single alike—be they relatives or friends of the men in the family.

The married women of the younger generation have the greatest liberty in associating with men who visit their homes, whether they are older or of the same age. Most men of this generation regard the veil as unnecessary in the presence of men who are allowed to enter the house frequently, unless such men are of "a backward mentality and object to meeting women," as one informant put it. However, tolerance requires a reciprocal arrangement in the case of two friends. Unless each of them allows his wife to be seen unveiled by the other, the traditional code is upheld by both.

The relatively greater freedom of married women to veil or not to veil relates to the shift of authority over their behavior from their fathers or elder brothers to their husbands. An unmarried women's laxity in this regard damages her family's name and reduces her chances of getting a "good" husband. Once she is married, it is her husband's privilege to decide how, where, and when she should veil herself, a decision usually taken in recognition of currently acceptable limits.

An unmarried younger-generation woman does not appear unveiled to anyone who is her potential husband (except kinsmen who grew up with her), not even to friends of the man of the house whom she may have met abroad. To act otherwise would jeopardize the reputation of her family; "showing off" one's daughter or sister invites malign gossip.

The entire question of the degree of liberty available to an unmarried woman, of whatever generation, is something closely tied to community judgment. The unmarried woman is perhaps more than any other person felt to be under the protection of community norms. Concomitantly, her acts are likely to be subject to the closest possible scrutiny.

Ultimately, whenever a person's conduct comes under such inspection, either open or concealed, invoking the will of Allah lends indisputable authority to one's opinion, which shows the role of ideology in shaping human behavior. Religious dogma and social norms, in theory if not always in practice, are inextricably fused in Jiddah society. But that fusion is not immutable. Transformations in people's conduct have their resonance in modification of the ideology. An action judged sinful at some earlier time now becomes devalued in significance in being seen as, at most, shameless. There is a major difference between sinning, which is to reject Allah's eternal authority, and being shameless. To be sure, shameless behavior is a violation, but of a social norm which is changeable and not of a religious one which is sacrosanct. What earlier may have been deemed an outrage in total infringement of divine strictures comes to be viewed as an unfortunate lapse that cannot be helped because that is the way it is with today's "modern generation."

Yet, in spite of changing social mores, the domestic world of the elite families continues to be deeply affected by Islam in both its great and little traditions. No house is without a copy of the Qur'an and a prayer rug. Even families which do not ordinarily keep to a strict religious regimen follow orthodox practice during periods of religious elaboration, such as Ramadan, the month of fasting. While women are excluded from participating in publicly performed Islamic rituals, with the exception of the minor pilgrimage to Macca (*'umrah*), they devoutly observe their religious duties within the house. However, because of their illiteracy, most women, especially those of the older generation, are ignorant of the literate and exegetic aspects of Islam. This ignorance explains the difference in performing standard rituals between men and women and the women's view that it is the men who "really know" about religious matters, so that their advice is to be sought and followed. In actual practice, at least the older women still believe in the efficacy of a variety of little rituals, such as wearing amulets and making vows to the Prophet and saints, that have survived the imposition of the Wahhabi reformation[6] in the Hijaz following its conquest by 'Abd al-'Aziz ibn Sa'ud in 1926.[7]

The Saudi government regarded the enforcement of adherence to pure, i.e., Wahhabi, Islamic teachings as its religious duty and, in time, utilized the mass media to teach the people the "proper" performance of religious rituals. Even today 70 percent of radio and television programs aim at religious indoctrination. Public and private schools socialize students into their role as informed and practicing Muslims. Although this policy has given common knowledge of religious beliefs and rituals to men and women alike, it has also increased the differences in religious knowledge between generations. The older generation, set in its pre-Wahhabi ways, has heard the mass media on the proper performance of the rituals without necessarily coming to terms with and internalizing the new ways. The middle and especially younger generations, for their part, have not only heard about these things but have unquestioningly accepted them as the correct ones.

Born and raised in a different religious climate (similar to the one described by Hurgronje for Macca),[8] the older women used to follow practices now declared heretical. For years they continued many of them in secret, only gradually accepting the Wahhabi dogma as it was taught to them by their husbands or literate daughters. As one old informant told me: "In the old days religious instruction was not available to us. We did not know what the girls of today know. We had no books, and we could not read. We had no television or radio to hear religious teachings. Since Ibn Sa'ud's rule people have become enlightened about religious matters; but look how the young ones of today have no fear of Allah and don't follow His orders."

Unlike their mothers, most women of the middle generation are literate and have, indeed, a better knowledge of the scriptural tradition of Islam, although they did not acquire this knowledge from formal schooling, as their daughters have done, especially after the opening of public girls' schools in Jiddah after 1960. For the practices of the past that are still retained these women have adopted interpretations and justifications that are in line with current religious teachings.

In all families studied, religious fastidiousness had declined over the three generations. The trend in all probability is due partly to the influence of historical events and partly to stages in the life cycle of these men and women. All older men perform the five obligatory prayers, and most of them pray in a mosque on each occasion. The majority of men in the middle generation still perform all obligatory prayers but restrict their visits to the mosque to Friday noon. Only about half of the younger-generation men pray regularly, though less than five times a day and only on Friday when they visit the mosque.

Similarly, the older women do all the obligatory prayers, often promptly at the call for prayer, an act thought to bring greater reward from Allah. They are also meticulous about avoiding pollution, carefully observing the required ablutions and paying special attention to their prayer rugs and prayer shawls. Whereas most middle-generation women pray five times daily, they seldom do so promptly. The younger-generation women pray even less regularly. Most of them actually restrict regular praying to the month of Ramadan and, for most of the time, pray only some obligatory prayers, neglecting others.

In matters of prayer, Islamic norms suggest that no distinctions separate the sexes. But while the spiritual equality of men and women implies identical religious duties, a number of injunctions restrict a woman's participation in these rituals. Not only is she barred from praying in a mosque (other than the mosques in Macca and Madina), but the exercise of her religious duties at home is also circumscribed by conventions that reflect her segregated position at home.

Therefore, although communal prayer is more greatly rewarded by Allah than individual prayer, men and women rarely pray together except during Ramadan, when some families join in the special Ramadan *tarawih* prayer. At the communal prayer the men form a straight line closely behind the prayer leader, and the women form their own line at some distance behind the men. Only men may, and do, raise their voices during some stages of prayer, whether praying alone or communally. Schoolbooks say that it is possible for a woman to take the role of prayer leader for other women (without standing ahead of the line), but most women are uncertain about this possibility. Furthermore, unlike a man, a woman must wear special attire for prayer, a large shawl that leaves only her face bare.

But, for all the generations and for both sexes, annual religious rituals, such as those associated with Ramadan and the pilgrimage, usually initiate a period of intense religious and social activity. Ramadan, for example, has three important consequences for these elite families. First, religious activity mounts and is expressed in greater participation by individuals who do not practice Islamic teaching during the rest of the year. Second, the belief that Ramadan is an especially blessed month results in the distribution of financial aid, which constitutes a regular income for a considerable number of people who are financially dependent on these families—as will be described below. Third, social visits activated during this month maintain ties with close *ahl* and *arham* and are occasions for family heads to renew ties with kinsmen whom they rarely visit during the year. Furthermore, the exchange of visits among men in the feast ending the month of Ramadan provides the only opportunity for men to visit formal acquaintances and maintain their relationships.

As in some other Islamic countries, Ramadan in Saudi Arabia alters the routine pace of life, shifting activities from day to night. The society has no accommodations for those who do not observe fasting. No public restaurants or groceries are open during the day. Individuals who declare their nonconformity are rare. Medical excuses are usually acceptable, but public display of nonobservance of fasting is strongly criticized.

Fasting consists of abstention from food, drink, smoking, and sexual intercourse from dawn to sunset. After sunset and until dawn all these activities are resumed. Sick people and menstruating women are exempt from fasting but must compensate by fasting the same numbers of days, and where ill health bars fasting altogether, a Ramadan day not fasted must be compensated for by feeding the needy. There is no agreement among women on the number of needy to be fed—those who have to do it consult men for details.

Generally, however, older- and middle-generation women observe the fast strictly even at the expense of great physical discomfort. Women of the younger generation do not conform as readily but are often careful to provide a "legitimate" excuse for not fasting. In addition to fasting, men and women alike in these families observe *tarawih* prayer, read the Qur'an, and devote some time of the day to religious activities and to listening to the religious programs which the Saudi broadcasting service devotes to fasting and other related matters.

Ramadan day, for women as well as for men who are independent businessmen, begins near noon prayer. With the noon prayer, the house slowly stirs to life. The older women "read" the Qur'an, do some sewing, and attend to the house. Some of the men either go back to sleep after prayer or leave the house for about two hours of work, returning home shortly before sunset.

Activity increases following the afternoon prayer, when everybody in the house is awake, some preparing meals to break the fast, others reading the Qur'an, and others invoking Allah by using the rosary, with still others listening to religious programs on the radio.

As sunset draws closer the household gets busier until the radio announces sunset and the call to prayer. At this moment, all family members congregate near the food area, domestic servants as well, with men and women in their own quarters. Following the traditions associated with the Prophet, the fast is broken with water (or juice) and dates. The people then perform the sunset prayer before sitting down to the breakfast meal.

After the first meal and until evening prayer, family members gather around the television, sipping tea and conversing. Afterwards, the men leave for work or on visits to friends, and most do not return before 1:00 A.M. Similarly, women begin their social calls between 9:00 and 10:00 P.M. and are always home for the last meal before the next fasting day. This meal is usually served shortly before dawn. Many do not sleep before performing the morning prayer.

Until the last two decades women of the older generation did not exchange visits during Ramadan except with the kinsmen of their natal family and possibly with a close circle of friends. An old informant explained: "We rarely went out, first because women did not go out much in those days, and second because we had so much to do during that month that we could not go out. We had to sew clothes for all the houseold and clean the house for the feast [ending Ramadan]."

Now, however, the beginning of Ramadan initiates a period of visits exchanged with "close" and "distant" kinsmen, as well as the formal visits described earlier as *wu'ud*. The earlier days of the month are reserved for congratulatory visits between *ahl* and *arham* initiated by the younger and returned by the older. Failure to pay these visits is viewed as negligence of the other party's rights and thus has adverse affects on the relationship between the two parties.

The end of Ramadan is celebrated by a feast extending for four days. The first three days are marked by daily congratulatory visits among men to *ahl* and *arham*, friends and acquaintances. All these visits must be returned before the feast ends, with the result that often men do not see their host (who would be on his round of visits) and so leave a card proving their visits.

In the afternoon some of the middle- and most of the younger-generation couples pay their visits together to houses of *ahl* and *arham*. These congratulatory visits are greatly valued and are especially observed with kin no matter how distant or how rarely visited. Among women, congratulatory visits are largely limited to kin and possibly close friends. They do not begin until the fourth day of the feast ending Ramadan, when the rush of men's visits ends. This is largely because supervision of their houses and preparation for men guests are given priority and take up the better part of the day.

Since Ramadan is considered an especially blessed month, some rituals which can be performed at any time of the year are popularly observed during this month. Of all these, the most important is the *'umrah*, the minor pilgrimage, which these families undertake at least once during the month of fasting.

The rituals for it are essentially the same as those of the main pilgrimage, which a Muslim is required to make once in his or her lifetime. In both the minor and main pilgrimages, men and women observe the same tabus, wear the same attire, and perform the same rituals in the Haram, the mosque at Macca. The basic rituals of the pilgrimage relevant here include donning a special garment, which differs for women and men. For the former, it includes a long shawl covering the head and body (and in the past even the face). For the man, it consists of two pieces of unsewn cloth: one covers the body below the waist, and the other covers the chest and one shoulder, leaving the other bare. It should be noted that this attire is worn after a washing ritual during which people bathe as a sign of intent to begin the pilgrimage. Then the garment is donned and a special prayer made which again signals the intent to proceed on the pilgrimage. Once these steps are taken, the individual enters into a period of tabu observance until all the rituals are completed. Tabus common to men and women include abstention from sexual contact, a prohibition against killing or hurting animals except in self-defense, injunctions against deracinating plants or trees, and refraining from any show of anger. The attire may not be changed, hair may not be cut, and men must not shave nor women beautify their faces. These tabus end with the completion of the rituals, and the ending is symbolized by cutting an amount of hair as a preliminary to undoing the pilgrimage attire.

Common to both pilgrimages is the visit to the mosque at Macca to perform the circumambulation ritual around the Ka'bah (the black cube in the main courtyard); and for the walk between two sacred locations in the back of the Haram, which is done seven times. Both rituals are accompanied by recitation of standard formulas which include invocations for forgiveness, entry into heaven, good health, loyal children, contented parents, and the like.[9]

The differences between the main and minor pilgrimages are slight. First, the intention for all acts is verbalized for the minor pilgrimage alone. Second, the minor pilgrimage ends with the completion of rituals at the Haram, when the "opening" of pilgrimage attire completes the period of tabu observance. In the main pilgrimage, individuals then move to other locations for a series of ritual observances that extend over two to three more days.

Though in theory, as with the main pilgrimage, the minor pilgrimage is not a possibility for women who are not accompanied by a *mahram* (a male relative whom she may not marry), many women of different generations perform it without a male companion. A few household heads go with their women on the minor pilgrimage. The rest go alone or with other male kin, leaving the women to accompany each other. Although there is no definite pattern to the groups of women who take the trip together, many do so with some *ahl* or with *arham* with whom they maintain a greater degree of interaction. Some women may accompany their "close friends" on a minor pilgrimage. All arrange for their domestic servants to make at least one minor pilgrimage during Ramadan. Since Macca is only 74 miles southeast of Jiddah, the trip is made in a few hours and does not lead to an overnight stay in Macca.

Once again, it is possible to see tension between the norm and the practice in regard to the issue of accompaniment. If the requirement of *mahram* accompaniment for women on the major and minor pilgrimages has lapsed, we need to ask why this is so. Indeed, as in the case of veiling in private places, even older-generation women have come to disregard this norm. Or, it is more accurate to say that they have reinterpreted it as part of a strategy to provide themselves with greater mobility and therefore autonomy. The principle of accompaniment remains, but it now applies to women co-pilgrims who are relatives or even friends. It is, however, true that breach of the *mahram* rule during the *hajj* requires compensation. In this case, the compensation is in the form of the sacrificing of an extra animal. This process is not a change in accepted ideology that has permitted initiative on the part of women; instead, it represents the gradual dissolution of the traditional patrilocal extended-family household and a slackened religious fervor among the younger men, who may not care to assume the burden of organizing a pilgrimage for their families.

One explanation for the change is that it is more convenient for both men and women to drop the male *mahram* requirement. As occupational and business routines become more complex in terms of time, travel, commitments to attend meetings, etc., it may be that men's schedules make it increasingly difficult to accommodate the *mahram* rule. A second explanation for the trend may be that it provides women with an additional social occasion to renew ties.

A final point that bears mentioning in connection with the pilgrimage is that the feast following it is an occasion when some men and women remember their deceased relatives. In doing so, they sacrifice a sheep on behalf of a deceased father, mother, sibling, and less commonly, a relative of the grandparental generation. Members of the younger generation, however, have become less involved in these acts. This may, especially for the women, be a sign of their general lack of involvement in the traditional networks of their parents, as we shall see in chapter 4.

The religious belief that "good deeds" are more greatly rewarded by Allah during Ramadan than at any other time brings philanthropic activity to a climax during this month. Paying an annual religious charity tax of 2½ percent on capital and earnings (the *zakat al-mal*) is a duty outlined in the Qur'an. It is left entirely to individual initiative without government interference. All the families distribute the alms tax annually to needy *ahl, arham,* friends, and others. Generally, the household head allocates a portion of the alms tax money to his wife for distribution to needy women. Though ideally this is to be distributed to all those in need, actually it is donated to the same individuals every year. Inclusion on the list of beneficiaries is permanent, and the recipients come around to collect their share. Hence, though in theory it is haphazard almsgiving, in fact it constitutes a regular source of income for those individuals on a family's list. Since the social world of women is largely limited to the domestic scene and since all these families interact with each other, beneficiaries appear often on the list of several families. Although most families do not fully disclose their alms tax list to others because it is viewed as charity that must not be publicized, women often volunteer to friends and relatives names of needy people to be added to a list where additional money is available for distribution. If, for example, the wife of a poor fisherman is on the alms tax list of family X and during her visits to this family she meets women from other families, she may be included on their lists, even if she does not cultivate friendship with them. Often, the lady of the house recommends her name to other friends whom she knows to be distributing alms tax, or *haqq* Allah, "that which belongs to God," as it is called by women.

Over and above the alms tax and almsgiving, heads of households provide all their dependents with a minimum of one full outfit that constitutes their annual clothing ration. The wealthier families increase this and also extend it to include the families of their servants as well as other poor women who have friendship ties with the women of the household.

Conclusions

This chapter has focused upon a number of aspects of household life as they reflect the segregation of women from men in these *ahl al-balad* elite families. It has also traced the extension of segregation in the performance of various religious rituals. Changes in both areas have also been described. Taken together, the practices and rituals examined here—in the context of male-female and female-female relationships—suggest an interrelationship of norm observance and strategies to reformulate some of the norms. Men and women in their household relations seek to improve their positions by adhering to a variety of cultural norms and following certain strategies to widen the scope of their autonomy. In general, men and women of the younger generation seem to have been more successful in doing this than their counterparts in both older and middle generations. One may describe this in terms of their greater tactical mobility. Also, within the middle and younger generations, the power of women has increased as a result of such things as increasing educational opportunities, a heightened awareness of where they would like to live, travel, and a general diffusion of more "modern" norms from the outside world. These trends may be witnessed in :

(1) Movement away from viripatrilocal to neolocal residence patterns
(2) Changes in veiling requirements
(3) Changes in pilgrimage participation
(4) Reduced almsgiving.

In general, then, members of the younger generation have gained a better understanding of their rights and privileges under Islamic law, so that the women of this generation have experienced greater opportunities for extending control over their lives. These opportunities are increasingly utilized by such women not only vis-à-vis their men but also in connection with their relations with one another. As the following chapter will show, that understanding came at a time when exogenous culture change encouraged potentially far-reaching changes in domestic relationships.

NOTES

1. Hurgronje describes the complex organization of the profession of pilgrimage agents in Macca in the latter part of the nineteenth century and

points to the substantial income it generated for the people involved in Jiddah. See Snouck Hurgronje, *Mekka*, pp. 24–29, 78–80.

2. Fatima Mernissi, *Beyond the Veil*, pp. 3 ff, 83 ff.

3. Also, Daisy Hilse Dwyer, *Images and Self-Images*, pp. 152–53.

4. Clifford Geertz, Hildred Geertz, and Lawrence Rosen, *Meaning and Order in Moroccan Society*, p. 332.

5. Melford E. Spiro, *Children of the Kibbutz*, pp. 347 ff.

6. Two fundamental Wahhabi tenets are absolute monotheism with rejection of acts implying polytheism, such as tomb visitations or saints' worship; and condemnation of innovations affecting the original teachings of Islam. See George Rentz, "Wahhabism."

7. For a description of this conquest see Lawrence P. Goldrup, "Saudi Arabia, 1902–1932," pp. 367–93.

8. Hurgronje, *Mekka*, passim.

9. For details, see Altorki, "Religion and Social Organization."

CHAPTER THREE

ROLES AND ROLE CONFLICTS

S EGREGATION of men and women in the home is accompanied by a pervasive separation of the roles of husband and wife. For the older generation, there were few spheres in domestic living in which the division of labor did not consign different tasks and privileges to husband and wife. For the middle and younger generations certain formerly distinct roles have become fused, as the spouses have begun to share activities and to cooperate in making decisions, especially those affecting the upbringing of their children.

Such cooperation in decision-making runs counter to an earlier set of beliefs that centers on the concept of *'aql,* "reason." According to this older ideology, men are not only physically but mentally superior to women, despite the Qur'anic view that women are equal to men in religious duty and reward. In fact, women are considered "lacking in reason (*'aql*) and religious observance." This view is based on the physical nature of women, whereby the biological condition of menstruation puts them in a state of ritual pollution which suspends religious duties of prayer and fasting. This brings a temporary lapse in religious obligations not experienced by men. Such conditions endure for women until they reach menopause. Hence, no matter how devout they are, they are still viewed by men and view themselves as failing in religious duty.

'Aql refers to the faculty of understanding, rationality, judiciousness, prudence, and wisdom. Such faculties are seen by women and men alike to be found more in men than in women, especially when such attributes relate to judgment. It is, however, expected that women can and do exercise *'aql* in controlling their own behavior, in running the affairs of their household, in their relations with others (especially within the extended family), in keeping the love

and attention of their husbands, in tolerating their husbands' short-comings and forgiving them when conflicts arise.

Curiously, it is this last meaning where women are expected to have *'aql* and are recognized to have it. But in regard to *'aql* as the ability to be judicious, women and men alike see the faculty as more befitting a man than a woman. This is basically a result of the nature of women, believed to be one of extremes that cloud judgment and, in fact, may lead to radical swings in behavior. Hence, some men and women argue that Allah, in His mercy, gave man and not woman the power to divorce. "If women had it, we would have more broken families, as women's emotional natures would lead them, in fits of anger, to break up their homes," as one woman informant put it.

Similar beliefs about *'aql* are described for Morocco by Dwyer.[1] There, however, *'aql* is seen by women to begin for girls at the early age of about seven and for boys around age twenty. Theoretically, for men *'aql* grows with the responsibility that marriage brings, but in effect it has no starting point. However, most men reach their quota of *'aql* no earlier than forty, or mature adulthood, when men are perceived to have achieved sufficient capacity to deal with the complex problems of social existence.[2] It is the perception of men that they possess greater *'aql* than women, while women, in men's view, have more *nifs*, desires of the flesh. This is a view that is partially accepted by women, who, however, disagree that men have less *nifs* than they do.

The Jiddah elite ideology, which is corroborated by Moroccan data, thus envisions *'aql* in the context of a development cycle. In both cases, a deficiency of *'aql* among women is attributed to a closer identification of women with carnal traits. A new development among younger-generation elite women is an enlargement of the domain of *'aql* for them. If they manifest *'aql* in regard to the inner realm of the household, then they can also acquire the ability to make important decisions affecting their lives more generally speaking. In other words, these younger-generation women are increasingly redefining *'aql* in ways that articulate with the emerging social individuality of women. Yet, in the final analysis, women of all three generations seem to agree that it is truly only with menopause that they attain their full quota of *'aql,* believed then to be proximate to that possessed by men.

In many respects, the Jiddah case not only corroborates Moroccan data but bears out the more general considerations brought out by Ortner in her discussion of women's identification with the realm of nature.[3] According to her analysis, the devaluation of women is a universal fact in all societies. Women's identification with the realm of nature—a lower order of human experience— rather than with the realm of culture explains their subordinate status. For culture, a higher realm of experience, is actually the arena for regulating and transcending the "overall processes of the world and life. If nature is the realm of disorder, then human beings must try to turn natural conditions to their own purposes and thereby triumph over them." As Ortner puts it, "Since it is always culture's project to subsume and transcend nature, if women were considered part of nature, then culture would find it 'natural' to subordinate . . . them."[4]

The Jiddah case suggests that Ortner's argument is valid that women seem to be ordinarily perceived as actors in the domain of nature. That domain is the locus of irrational forces and physically unregulated currents that challenge human societies. The reasons for women's greater identification with such a domain have to do with their physiology, the social role they play as the ballasts of the domestic unit, and, finally, the psychological view of them as the embodiments of the *concrete* and the *immediately present* (rather than the abstract and the rational, with which men are more readily identified). Thus, women are seen to have less reason, are viewed as more temperamental, less able to control themselves, more subject to the constraints of biological processes, and thereby likely to be at least temporary causes of ritual pollution against whom the community must be sheltered. Restitution of reason for women comes with menopause.

Given this framework for the interrelationship between men and women, it is now fitting to investigate the roles of husband and wife. The ideology juxtaposes these roles in asymmetrical but complementary positions. The man carries the full financial responsibility for the welfare of his wife and children. His wife is responsible for looking after the needs of the children, and especially if her husband is also the head of the household, she must oversee the daily domestic routine of preparing and serving meals and of keeping the house in good order. A wife's less tangible but still essential duty concerns the protection of her husband's name, a duty best met by obeying her husband's commands, particularly those affecting her social conduct in and outside the house. By observing her husband's orders, a wife protects his good name, i.e., his reputation, and the honor of her own lineage, on whom blame would fall if she were to violate customary rules of propriety. Women recognize the double jeopardy entailed in breaking the code of modesty. For example, a man can disassociate himself from an erring wife by divorcing her. Her own kinsmen have no such option, and their standing in the community irrevocably depends on the virtuous conduct of their daughters.

Any violation of the modesty code brings 'ayb, shame, but the nature of acts considered shameful has changed. For the older-generation women avoiding 'ayb meant to abide strictly by their husbands' orders, however whimsical they might have appeared. As one old woman put it: "A woman must obey her husband and show him respect. If he says that she is not to go shopping, then she should not. She should not unveil to any man, if her husband does not want her to do so, even if the man is his brother." This kind of sentiment does not mean that the older women always practiced what they so readily acknowledge as the duty of a wife, although the identification of unconditional obedience to a husband as a religious duty made any *publicly* shown defiance very rare. Failing to veil in the presence of older male servants when the husband was not at home was one breach that not a few of the older women frequently dared to commit. The continued practice of non-orthodox Islamic rituals, such as holding shamanistic curing ceremonies and celebrating saints' days, also encouraged women of this generation to ignore their husbands' wishes. Older-generation women claim that absolute patriarchy ruled their homes. This may not actually have been categorically true but will suffice here as a generalization.[5]

Withal such absolute patriarchy began to be modified even in the older generation as women reacted to the inconvenience they encountered in habitually interacting with older male servants in their homes and having to veil before them. The solution they hit upon, simply ignoring the husband's wishes unless he was present, in effect took the initiative to modify a norm, and became accepted practice.

Women of the middle and younger generations are less ready to grant men unrestrained authority. For them, the voluntary submission to a husband's will is contingent on the perceived "reasonableness" of his demands. Thus, they evade an order not to go out shopping, now that the busy downtown district affords considerably more anonymity than it did in the past. But none would dare question a husband's right to determine the limits of her interaction with other men. For example, where a man permits his wife to appear unveiled in the presence of men invited to the house, any show of familiarity or physical contact with them is still not tolerated in any of the families. Joking, discussing, or even alluding to sexual matters and wearing dresses considered seductive remain serious infractions of the modesty code.

Open defiance of her husband's wishes is still considered scandalous. Women of all three generations acknowledge a man's exclusive right to control his wife's movements outside the house. In this respect, however, old conventions have become more flexible. For example, one old woman, who was required to ask her husband's permission every time she wanted to leave the house, told me:

> When my daughter grew up and married, she talked to her father about my outings and persuaded him that times have changed and that I, having grown old, should no longer require his permission. Since then, I have not asked his permission for all my outings during the day, but I have continued to do so when I wanted to go out at night, to a wedding, for example, and I expected to return home late.

Ideally, a woman must secure her husband's permission for any outing, even for a visit to her natal family, and older women remembered that they were allowed such visits only to attend important occasions such as a death, a wedding, the birth of a child, or a religious feast. In actual behavior, however, the mobility of most women was and is not entirely dependent on their husbands' decisions. Many of the older women told me that they often went out behind their husbands' backs to make social calls or to attend celebrations at the homes of friends, when their husbands were away from the house or the sleeping arrangements permitted their absence to go unnoticed—a matter more easily managed if they had an older daughter who could attend to the father.

On the other hand, if a man discovered his wife's disobedience, he could reprimand her and report her to her own father, who in many cases would support his right to dictate his wife's movements. If a woman went to her father's house to protest against her husband's reproach, her father usually sent her back to her husband, often without waiting for him to come and fetch her.

Though still recognizing a husband's rights in this matter, most women of the middle and younger generations have managed to escape strict supervision. Rather than obtaining his permission each time they leave the house, they tend to acknowledge his authority by informing him of their whereabouts before going out. However, if a woman fears that her husband will object to her plan, she succeeds in transgressing his orders without repercussions by concealing her outing. Such disobedience is not so much seen as a dishonest act as it is considered the only way of obtaining a degree of freedom that has become accepted by other families of her class, and she may talk about it lightly and freely with other women without fear of criticism.

Nonetheless, the younger women, who appear to have more freedom of movement than their mothers ever had, are still restrained by their husbands' whims. The restraint does not seem to be diminished in a marriage where both spouses have been educated in Egypt or in the United States—a situation exemplified by the following incident:

> After the feast ending the month of Ramadan many people visit Madina. Nadia was invited on the telephone by her mother to travel there with her natal family. She accepted the invitation without consulting her husband, since she had gone on such trips several times before. However, her husband, who had been present during the telephone conversa-

tion but had said nothing at the time, forbade her to leave as she was packing her suitcase because she had neglected to seek his permission before accepting the invitation and had thereby defied his authority. Nadia did not go to Madina, and when I questioned her about the matter, she admitted: "I know I was wrong not to tell him before accepting, but," she continued, "why did he have to remain silent until the night of the departure?" When I later mentioned this case to informants of all three generations, they unhesitantly expressed their admiration for the "reasonable [*'aqilah*, from *'aql*] girl who respects her husband's word." Commenting on her husband's behavior, older and younger women alike said he had no "right" to delay until the end before informing his wife. Moreover, she was going with her mother, so what was the harm in that?

In general, a wife is expected to conform to her husband's social demands unless they involve a violation of Islamic teachings or valued tradition. The following two cases describe the view concerning a wife's relation to her husband that prevails among the families today:

Ahmad, who belongs to the middle generation, was educated abroad. After his return he married his father's sister's daughter, who had no formal schooling. Within a few years he reached an important position in the administration. As an "educated" man, Ahmad was not strict about the veiling of his wife, and he often had mixed gatherings in his house. His wife, unable to overcome the traditions she was brought up to value, found it difficult to adapt to this style of life. Her inexperience and lack of schooling made her ill at ease with the kinds of friends whom her husband, by virtue of his position, was meeting. Ahmad encouraged her to take private lessons in English and Arabic, but she declined. When Ahmad pronounced her once-divorced,[6] her women friends and acquaintances individually empathized with her, especially since she had three children, but communal opinion favored her husband. At a social gathering which discussed the case, a middle-aged woman expressed its consensus when she exclaimed: "She is wrong. Times have changed, and men now expect that their wives be 'modern.' Why, then, do we get upset when our men go to Egypt and Lebanon to get their wives? If this is the kind of life her husband leads, she must blend with it without losing respect. If her husband wants her to get educated, she must do that. If she doesn't, he will leave her and marry a woman better suited to his style of life. His wife will be the loser."

However, while a man may demand that his wife acquire an education, a married woman is by no means free to attend school except with her husband's consent.

Before her marriage, a young woman had obtained a high school degree in Cairo. Following the birth of a son, she wanted to enroll in King 'Abd al-'Aziz University in Jiddah. Her husband objected to her plan, and when she insisted, he threatened her with divorce. When the news was discussed in a social gathering, a middle-aged woman said: "Women are going mad these days. If her husband doesn't want her to get educated, she should stay home. After all, how can she leave her child and go to the university?"

The issue in dispute was the same in both cases, and so was the conservative reaction on the part of the women's community. The issue, however, was not whether a woman should or should not be educated, but whether or not she must accede to her husband's demands.

The role of a good wife which the proverbial "reasonable girl" is obliged to assume upon her marriage has, in fact, changed little over the three generations as far as it concerns attending to a husband's needs. Speaking of the past, one old woman explained:

A wife attended to her husband's clothes, to his food, observed his schedule so that food was ready when he wanted it. She got him his food to eat first, and then she ate with the women if they were the type of family where husband and wife didn't eat together. In our days a woman would even clean her husband's shoes and present them to him.

Today middle- and younger-generation women, by and large, oblige their husbands in the same manner. They give utmost care to the husband's hours for serving food and they may personally attend to his clothes regardless of whether a servant could do that. They know that their failing in these tasks may induce a man to seek another wife who would give him the care and attention he demands. The one exception among the families was a young woman who did the jobs expected of her at her leisure. Other women criticized her for neglecting her husband and regarded her unworthy of his support. They regarded his unvoiced grievances and cool temper as reflecting unusual restraint.

A woman's duties also included supervision of her household and keeping expenditure within limits that her husband could afford. In the older generation the male head of the household usually controlled the budget—rarely did a woman—even if the household included a married son. However, more and more wives of the younger generation control the household budget, and within its limits they have the freedom to run the house as they please. They supervise domestic servants, especially the female domestic helpers, whom they can hire and dismiss.

A man's needs include his sexual desires, and any reluctance shown by his wife provides him with a socially acceptable excuse to look for other women. Popular religious beliefs, common among women of the older generation, support a husband's unmitigated right to sexual satisfaction. One old woman recounted: "I was told by my father's sister, who lived with us in my father's house, that if a husband desires his wife and she refuses him, the angels will curse her through the night. It is tabu for a woman to refuse her husband. Because I fear Allah, I always remembered her warning." On the other hand, a woman would act shamelessly if she were to initiate intercourse, even though she, too, has an acknowledged right to sexual satisfaction. In fact, people belive that if a man neglects his wife, Allah will not forgive him, even if she does.

Fertility is valued in men and women. It is the duty of a wife to bear children for her husband. Most older-generation couples had an average of seven children. Infant mortality was remarkably high at that time; all the families studied lost a minimum of one to two infants. Over the three generations there was a drop both in the number of children (an average of four children for middle-generation couples and of two for younger-generation couples) and in the mortality rate. The two trends are clearly related. They have resulted mainly from improved health conditions since the establishment of the current government and from a modified concept of raising children. Since some middle-generation women and most younger-generation women directly supervise the children, they are less dependent on nannies[7] and invest more time and energy with their children. Within the last decade, however, and with the economic boom that Saudi Arabia has experienced, the number of foreign servants and nannies has increased in the country as a whole, and among the elite in particular. Mothers of the younger generation now have at least one nanny, but they are still involved in taking care of their children.

By agreement between the spouses some middle- and younger-generation women use Western birth control methods, as they have little faith in the local methods which their mothers sometimes used. There is neither concern nor awareness on the part of men and women of the position of Islam regarding birth control. The women, however, are concerned about the side effects which the pill might have on their health. I have no cases where use of contraceptives was not endorsed and agreed upon by both spouses. This is probably due to the fact that by the time of fieldwork middle-generation women were between forty and fifty years of age and had grown, teenage children. Most of these mothers found it ridiculous to think of having babies when they should be thinking about finding spouses for their sons and daughters. A younger-generation woman who already has two or three children uses contraceptives because the mother does not wish to wear herself out bringing up another child, and the father is not certain that his income can guarantee a "good life" for a bigger family.

Bringing up and supervising children is the responsibility of both parents. However, socialization of boys and girls begins to differ around the age of seven to nine, or, as others say, "when a child's body starts to develop." The boy gradually moves to the men's quarters under his father's supervision. On the other hand, a daughter, by virtue of her restriction to the house, is socialized by her mother, older siblings, and other female relatives living in the house. They supervise her food and clothes, teach her appropriate modes of behavior and religious rituals, and train her for adult life. Though ideally the permission a girl needs for outings has to come from the father, it is the mother who controls her daughter's movements. One of the older-generation women told me, "When my daughters were young, their father did not mind their outings, especially to my family and his family [brother and cousins]. But I did not let them go even when he gave them permission. I did not want them exposed to just any company. Of course, they did not complain to their father." On the other hand, a mother could always find a way to circumvent her husband's wishes and collude with her daughters in facilitating visits to other homes. The father participated actively in the socialization of his male offspring only. There were always cases where the father's long absence or temporary residence abroad or even his submissive character brought his sons under their mother's supervision, leaving the husband as nominal figurehead. When this happened, the wife was either admired for "bringing up men in the absence of men" or regarded as interfering with her husband's responsibilities—for it was said that "no one can bring up a man except [another] man."

With middle-generation couples there has been an increasing overlap in the socialization of children; fathers supervise girls in religious teachings and mothers participate in decisions influencing their sons' education, travel, hours of absence from the house, etc. For example, in one family the father allowed his 18-year-old son a late night (midnight) once a week, but the mother insisted that his latest hour be 10:00 P.M. When the boy returned later than that, he was reprimanded by his mother in the presence of his father—and the boy was informed that 10:00 P.M. was the latest he could stay out. My intimate knowledge of the couple permits an interpretation of the wife's decision not as resulting from her dominant personality but rather as due to the longer time she spends with her children. Her husband's frequent travels leave her for many months of the year in a position of authority over both her sons and her daughters. Such assumption of a male function alters only slightly in the presence of her husband.

Any major decision regarding the children's health or education is ultimately in the hands of the father—who should provide the best care and schooling, including education for girls and boys in private schools, whether in Jiddah or abroad, and often extending through college. Yet I have observed young mothers taking such decisions during their husband's absence. Nowadays, young mothers with some schooling are even responsible for supervising their children's education, and I have observed young couples discussing together the kind of schools their children are to attend. Obviously, older-generation women had neither the knowledge nor the experience to participate in such discussions, which left them with little to argue about in their husband's decisions. Nevertheless, they had some say in matters concerning the education of their daughters, and their consent was always sought to sending their sons to schools abroad. Sometimes, if a mother refused to let her son go abroad, her husband heeded her wishes and sent the boy to a school in Jiddah, so that his mother would be spared the "heartache" of his departure and prolonged absence from home.

Younger-generation mothers expect their husbands to share in all the major responsibilities of caring for the children. Women often complain that "husbands don't give a hand in the house or even in changing the children's clothes or feeding them. The other day, after I fed our daughter, I asked my husband to wash her hands. He turned to me and said, 'Are you going to turn me into a woman? This is your job, not mine.' It's always like this—the only time they give help is when we are in a hotel in Europe."

Perhaps the notable thing about this story is not the man's rejection of his wife's request for assistance with the baby but her expectation that he would give assistance. In this case, one can observe the effort of a younger-generation woman to renegotiate the standards for her role vis-à-vis her husband. Put another way, what this Jiddah woman is actually doing is reaching out for greater independence from the ties that bind her to her domestic duties. At first blush, a request that her husband wash their child's hands seems insignificant. But, as the man himself implies in his refusal, a principle is involved here. Acceding to the request would possibly lead, down the road, to a shift in the man-woman relationship. The accumulation of discrete changes, after all, can lead to a basic transformation. These changes include a modified concept of raising children among the middle- and younger-generation men and women, the increased ability of women to discipline sons, supervise daughters' outings, and participate in decisions for the schooling of children. Individually, the force of such changes may not affect the asymmetry in the relationship between men and women. In their aggregate, however, they could temper that asymmetry.

Unlike a man, a wife who neglects her domestic duties risks her husband's either divorcing her or taking a second wife. When a woman does observe these duties and her husband still seeks other women, either for marriage or for extramarital relations, the woman will acquiesce in silent disapproval. Sexual fidelity is expected of a husband but rarely observed. Some men from the families studied had extramarital relations when they went on vacations outside Saudi Arabia. Without knowing the details, women tend to distrust men's claims to fidelity. Yet, they consider infidelity characteristic of the male sex and therefore unavoidable. Consequently, discretion being more valued than fidelity, extramarital affairs of men are tolerated almost as much as their premarital relations are accepted.

The fidelity of a wife is expected irrespective of her husband's behavior. In all the families studied, the fidelity of the wives was a principle that was strictly observed, and to my knowledge no infractions occurred. Infidelity on the part of women is viewed as a serious matter that compromises their honor and that of their families and husbands. Women of all three generations condemn female infidelity absolutely and reject the notion that a husband's unfaithful behavior releases them from the obligation to abide by community norms in this matter.

Men, of course, do have certain domestic duties and obligations, despite their greater prerogatives in other areas. A husband's responsibilities commit him to support his wife and children, provide his offspring with an education, be kind and attentive to his spouse, and be good to his affines.

Older-generation men typically provided all the needs of their household and gave their wives a sum of money for miscellaneous charges. Women controlled this sum and did not have to account for it unless the money ran out too soon.

Middle-generation women took over the task of handling household needs (a matter partially related to their mobility outside the house) and administering the household budget. Normally women received either a monthly or a bi-weekly sum. Again, detailed accounts are seldom given to husbands. Such matters become subject of discussion only when the money is exhausted unduly early. Allotments to wives cover salaries for women servants, but male servants (e.g., cooks, drivers, etc.) were usually handled by the husbands. Major expenditures, as, for example, airway tickets for vacations, school fees, hospital bills, were still settled by men.

With younger-generation women the arrangement remains roughly the same with a notable increase in their expenditure on clothes for themselves and their children. Such items are not covered by the monthly budget and have to be negotiated separately with husbands. Within the budget, as noted earlier, younger wives have considerable freedom to manage the household expenditures, but the money is always that of the husband.

A wife brings to her conjugal house a dowry which includes the complete furniture of two bedrooms, a salon, a livingroom, and a kitchen, as well as personal clothes to last her for at least a year. No further financial contributions to the household are expected of her, and her husband, alone, must look after the needs of the household to the full extent of his means. Even if a woman has property and income of her own, it would be *'ayb* to have her contribute to the family budget.

Among the families studied were those in which women had their own income. The source of such income was inheritance bequeathed to them through the application of the *shari'ah* law, which is strictly observed in Saudi Arabia. Usually, women inherit as either widows or daughters. While agnatic granddaughters, mothers, grandmothers, and sisters are also possible heirs, they either tend to be excluded by male relatives or their portions tend to be too small to be significant. Summarized briefly for the purposes of the present discussion, Islamic law grants the widow one-eighth of all the property; each son, irrespective of age, gets twice the share of each daughter. Despite their legal rights to inheritance women have no de facto control of their property and delegate its management to a brother, another agnate, or more recently to a husband.

Married women among the *ahl al-balad* elite who had their own income spent it on luxury items, such as jewelry or dresses for themselves and for their children. The women consider gems and expensive clothes to be paraphernalia of their status and believe

they enhance their husband's image in the community. In this belief, they are hardly wrong because gossip will quickly attribute any
poor quality in the clothes worn by a man's children and his wife to
regrettable poverty or to stinginess; in either case, he would not
measure up to a rank commensurate with his wife's.

As head of the household a husband shelters his family from the
burdens of the outside world. Men and women alike view this
arrangement as a protection of women from the distress and incon-
veniences of the public arenas and not as a restricting dependence
upon men. "Women were created weak," explained one old
woman. "They need men to protect them in the face of adversities.
No matter what a woman's wealth and education are, she cannot
live without the protection of a man."

Young women, however, while sharing the same sentiment, have
a more complex view of their position. The opinion of Nadia, the
educated wife of a man of the younger generation, reflected the
thinking of her age group when she said:

> I think that in our country men have a better position than
> women. On the other hand, the women don't have to be ex-
> posed to many inconveniences and to the struggle for living
> that they face in other countries. We don't have to slave to
> support a family—that burden falls on the man. We don't even
> have to be troubled by running around getting groceries or
> other necessities—the men do that. We do have our respon-
> sibilities, but they are different, though not less important,
> than those of men. Where would a family be without a mother
> in the house? What kind of children would a society have
> without the care given them by a full-time mother? It is not
> true that men control our lives. In the past, it was true. But I
> think that this thing depends on a woman's character. Take
> me, for example; I never felt that I was forced to do something
> because my husband wanted it—in fact, I often get him to do
> what I want. I don't do this by bossing him but in a clever way
> so he thinks that he controls the situation.

Since this Nadia is the same person who had to cancel a trip to
Madina with her own family owing to her husband's objection, one
could infer that her strategy of manipulating is not always successful. There is, however, no contradiction in principle between her

view of her own freedom and of her husband's rights. While these *rights* are nonnegotiable for her, she considers her *privileges* to cover a large field of action where she can, indeed, operate in a way that convinces her she is making decisions which suit her personal interests.

A man's responsibilities to support his household extend to any dependents who live in his house if they have no one else to look after them. With most of the families one finds female dependents who are not employed in the household. These women are usually the husband's *ahl* or *arham*, but there may also be old family friends or a long-time neighbor whose husband's death left her without a relative in Jiddah. In all cases the household head not only provides them with room and board and with clothing once or twice a year, but he also covers their medical expenses. Their acceptance into the household on a permanent basis can be seen as the functional equivalent of organized social security in other countries. Neglecting to offer such security to needy relatives and friends would harm the name of the family and brand the household head as a man who has no shame. Shameless acts for men would also include inadequate support for wife and children, neglect of his parents, immoral business dealings, and public displays in violation of community norms, such as drinking alcohol, gambling, and womanizing.

Upholding the family's good reputation requires, in addition, keeping an open and generous house. For example, lunch—the main meal—is always served in larger portions than required to feed the members of the household. One has to be prepared for informal guests who may come for lunch, and one may want to distribute some food to families known to be in need. In fact, most of the lunch guests are women from lower income groups who have maintained friendship ties with the host families, for ten to twenty years in some cases. To their less privileged friends, the families extend hospitality and support on occasions of crisis, such as death, illness, or the husband's unemployment. And once a year, they give these persons part of "Allah's dues." Until the recent past, many poor families depended on the daily delivery of lunch leftovers, and when the food did not arrive, they would go to the house and ask for it.

Few men of the younger generation who have established a neolocal household continue such displays of largesse. Their relatively small houses cannot so easily accommodate unannounced guests, and consequently there is usually less food left for distribution among the poor. They have other reasons, including economic and ideological, to all but abandon the traditional welfare system. Although their education and professional skills give them a considerable income, their few years in the world of business make wealth the promise of the future rather than the reality of the present. Their independent households simply cannot yet afford to match the expenditures of their fathers. *Zakat,* for example, is a tax on capital, and since most young men in the families are still less wealthy than their fathers, their payments of "Allah's dues" are necessarily much smaller. Those who have large incomes, such as engineers or merchants, may neglect to distribute alms because they may not care about the religious doctrine that defines these payments as an Islamic duty, although an eldest son, who will be the main heir to his father's prestige and the responsibilities that go with senior status, is more likely to comply. On the other hand, younger men readily continue to extend such favors as finding jobs for members of the families whose livelihood used to, or still does, depend on the charity of their fathers' household.

The responsibility for women's behavior is an important part of the general responsibilities of a household head. In practice this means that men directly enforce the norms of veiling for their women. As explained earlier, veiling is viewed by men and women alike as a religious injunction; any lapse is seen as sin, punished by Allah. Unveiling brings sin to the woman committing it and also to the household head, for it is viewed as part of a general responsibility for which he is accountable (here, to Allah).[8]

Veiling is also a social norm, enforcement of which is monitored by the most important male affecting a woman's behavior: namely, a husband or father (or surrogates thereof). It is therefore instructive to view the practice of veiling not only in terms of the religious rationale but as an expression of male authority over women's behavior, specifically their mobility outside the home.

On the whole, the younger-generation women are less limited by the veil than their grandmothers were. This correlates with a less asymmetrical power relationship that has slowly evolved between husband and wife over the three generations under study.

The changes in the ideology behind veiling, both religious and secular, occurred about the same time as the observance of veiling itself began to change. This, in turn, followed changes in the relationship between men and women. Thus, we find that although violation of the veiling norm is a major breach, it is really the social stigma resulting from *'ayb* that worries women. As a younger-generation woman put it to me:

> They say it is *harām* [tabu] to leave the hair uncovered and to wear short dresses, and even to wear perfume when one goes out. But I think this is a narrow-sighted explanation of religion. According to "them" most of what we do is *harām*. The Day of Judgment is another day. Besides, Allah is forgiving. These things [nonveiling] are *'ayb*. People eat you up with their tongues if you do it.

What constitutes shameless behavior has also changed over the three generations. With the older generation, veiling meant concealing all the face and body, except from male relatives one cannot marry. It also included—especially for Najdite men—a restriction on women not to raise their voices to a pitch that could be heard by male guests in the house. In the words of an older-generation woman:

> My husband was always scolding us [all women in the house] if he heard our voices in the men's side of the house. We liked singing, but we could only do that when he was out and stopped everything when it was time to expect him home. Even when we had [women] guests the singing would halt a little before he returned. My friends didn't mind, because they had to do that in their homes. Once, my husband returned early and heard our music and singing, and it made him so mad that I was scared to face him. I let my eldest daughter go to him to calm him down. He used to say that it is *harām* for a woman to raise her voice to a point where it is heard by men.

The pitch of a woman's voice is not discouraged because of its seductiveness to men; rather, it is because womens' voices should not be heard. The restriction on the voice of a woman has changed with middle- and younger-generation men who consider the views of the older men as "too strict and out of spirit for modern times."

Changes have also taken place in the isolation of women from potential husbands, both outside and inside the house. In these families when women go out, they are entirely dependent on cars. They do not walk, even if the distance does not merit a car ride. The only areas where they walk are isolated stretches outside the city or while shopping in the traditional market. A woman in a car is considered less exposed to men's eyes[9] than when she walks the streets of the city. This is particularly the case if the car drives her away from the busy business district, where all the men congregate and where the presence of a local woman draws attention. This explains why a woman removes the veil while she is in a car and why she strictly observes veiling in the traditional market. A younger-generation man who did not permit his wife to go shopping in Jiddah said:

> The traditional market is full of men who hang around scrutinizing women. I won't have my wife exposed to that. When she is outside that area, she can uncover her face; in fact, she sits near me in the car unveiled, and we go out for drives on Friday afternoon. Sure, other men see her near me, but it's a different situation; each car is moving toward its purpose and nobody is going to stand there and stare at her as they would in the traditional market.

Outside the house middle- and younger-generation women do not cover their faces except perhaps while shopping or in the downtown area. Only a few of these women (all the unmarried ones) cover the face while in a car outside the traditional market district. Today, with the spread of shopping centers all around the city, women of all generations go shopping. And in recent years, they do not cover their faces. The head shawl is carefully drawn over the hair, leaving the face bare.

Though all past marriage age, the unmarried women of the middle generation still observe the veil outside the house more closely than married women of their age group. The observance of the veil for a single woman is dictated by the father, or, in the case of his death, by an older brother. Married women of the younger generation adhere to the least strict observance of the veil outside the

They cover their heads only, leaving their faces bare when
_ e driven in autos outside the busy business district. They
also sit barefaced near their husbands when they are driven out to
places and when out for social calls, especially after sunset; they
often place the cloak near them without wearing it and leave it
behind when the get to their destination. The use of the cloak with
this generation is restricted to movement in the shopping area, and
the shawl is seldom placed on the face when they are out of the
busy district.

The house, as opposed to the world outside, provides a situation
where visual contact between men and women is controlled by
other means. Here, visual access of men to women is strictly controlled by the degree of kinship and friendship and by the status
relationship which obtains, as I have shown earlier in chapter 2.

Similar norms regulated visual access of one sex to the other
when they were living in other societies. For example, older- and
even middle-generation women usually avoided meeting Saudi
friends of their husbands while in Egypt or Lebanon or on trips to
Europe, where meeting Saudi men could not be avoided because
they stayed at the same hotel. Men and women did their entertaining and visiting separately, and older-generation men did not permit their wives or daughters past their teens to appear in front of
their male guests, especially Saudis—abroad and at home.

The middle-generation women, in the first five to ten years of
marriage, also passed through the phase of not appearing in front
of Saudi men who came to visit their husbands while in Egypt and
Lebanon. It is only since the 1970s that they have socialized with
Saudi friends of their husbands while abroad. These same women
now participate in social gatherings with married couples who are
"close friends" of their husbands even in Jiddah. However, the
majority of middle-generation women do not do so, even if they
have already met these men abroad, for upon return to Jiddah, the
pattern of social visits separates them.

Married women of the younger generation are allowed the greatest liberty of association with men who visit their homes. whether
such men are older than themselves or of the same age, they meet
with them, provided that the degree of interaction allows the husband to permit his wife such appearances.

This younger generation also shows an increasing tendency for husband and wife to pay joint visits to their friends. They entertain married couples, and such gatherings often include single men. In such gatherings, women are generally discreetly dressed, often in long dresses, and though they converse freely with men, they maintain decorous distance by abstaining from scandalous language—i.e., any open reference to sex.

Unmarried women of the younger generation do not appear unveiled to any potential husband who visits their house, except for single *ahl* who grew up with them and often saw them abroad when they were young. They do not appear unveiled in front of unmarried friends of the men in the house, and although they may have met abroad, they do not socialize in Jiddah. One married man of the younger generation told me, "Four years ago my sister was not married and was living with us. I did not receive mixed company then because I did not want people to start talking and saying 'He is showing his sister to other men so he can get her a husband.' It was after she married that I began to ask married couples over."

As the earlier discussion shows, veiling itself has become a subject of negotiation between the sexes. This does not mean that individuals bargain daily over the criteria for veiling, of course. But it indicates that changes have been occurring in the perception and behavior of men and women regarding veiling. As will be seen later in this chapter, such changes are generating conflicts between husband and wife, and, interestingly, between fathers, daughters, and the husbands of these daughters.

In all these changes, the ultimate authority rests with men. While it is the women who often initiate change, their behavior becomes acceptable only if backed by the authority of husband, father, or brother, who enforce the social norms. The projection of this authority into the larger society is reflected in the law, often enforced by the Saudi government, which forbids women, irrespective of age or status, to travel outside the kingdom without the written authorization of a male "guardian."

Parent-Child Relations

Children learn early in life to orient their behavior inside and outside the house by the rules that govern the safeguarding of the family's reputation. Similar to an obedient wife who must not question her husband's authority, a child of either sex is expected to submit to parental authority. Indeed, Islam condemns as sin any obstinate refusal to abide by parental orders. But even those who may not believe that hell awaits the deviant find social pressures toward conformity sufficiently strong to discourage rebellious acts and to curtail any open evasion of their duty to obey their parents.

There is no limit, either in Islam or in the value system of the community, to the realm of behavior where parents must be obeyed at all times (unless, of course, a parent's order violates canonic rules). This unlimited authority extends to the selection of a major in college no less than to the approval of a spouse.

As can be expected, the vast differences in world view and aspirations between the generations that emerged over the last forty years have made unmitigated submission to parental authority problematic. Beginning at the time when the now middle-aged men and women grew up, each age group has faced the problem of how to avoid sinful disrespect of their parents without giving up on trying to determine their own future, however small the stakes may have been by the norms acceptable today. Current norms of conduct are the result of a continuous process of negotiating changes without risking *ghadab,* the parent's wrath. This concept covers a wide range of responses to filial disrespect and disobedience, from momentary anger and longer-lasting discontent to outrage and, in extreme circumstances, to rejection. It may entail the expulsion of a son from his father's house. The sanction of *ghadab* derives its force from a combination of secular and mystical consequences: *ghadab* can lead to fission in the household by expelling the son, but it is also linked to Allah's *ghadab* and jeopardizes a person's soul no less than his worldly welfare. *Ghadab* cannot result in disinheritance, however, as that is inadmissible in Islam.

Quite apart from the threat of divine retribution, the values held by the elite families strongly support the religious norms of filial duty, at times exceeding them in practice. For example, Islamic law stipulates that financially capable children must care for their needy parents. According to the values of the community, that means providing much more than the bare necessities. Children who are considerably better off than their parents are expected to help them keep a home more comfortable than one which they can maintain by themselves. Both daughters and sons are required to assist their parents, but a daughter's support is secondary to that of a son and becomes essential only when she has no brother. In every one of the families studied in which a son was much wealthier than his parents, he supported them by fully maintaining the joint household or, if he had his own house, by contributing to their budget. A son who can afford to provide luxuries but stops at necessities is not respected as a man who treats his parents with due reverence. He does fulfill his duty, but he misses, the people believe, the rewards granted by Allah, not only on the Day of Judgment but also in this life, where reward accrues in profitable business, good health, and untroubled social relations. In a way, then, sons must demonstrate filial loyalty by supporting their parents financially. Daughters show their support mainly by rendering help in case of need, especially by personally taking care of their parents during sickness.

Children who support their parents win *rida*, or parental contentment, which, being the opposite of *ghadab*, also implies Allah's *rida*. However, children can forfeit their father's or mother's *rida* also by behaving in a querulous and obnoxious manner toward a sibling. In such a situation, a mother may invoke the sanction of *ghadab* to resolve a conflict between two of her children, as the following case illustrates:

Shafiqah, the third daughter in the family, had an argument with her eldest sister over the latter's interference in her movements. In the course of their argument, Shafiqah spoke insulting words to her sister, who, in turn, threatened to report her to their father. The mother, knowing that her husband favored the eldest daughter, feared that he might beat the younger daughter. Wanting to resolve the dispute before her husband's return for lunch, she urged Shafiqah to apologize to her elder sister. Realizing that her efforts were in vain, she threatened: "I, your mother, have been appealing to you for the last hour and you do not listen to my words. By Allah, my heart will harbor *ghadab* if you do not get up to apologize to your sister." On that note, she left the room. Women who were present approached the girl: "Please get up and do what your mother asks. You must not make her heart angry. Allah does not bless the *ghadibin* [those provoking their parents' *ghadab*], and they are doomed to hell." These admonitions changed Shafiqah's mind and she went to her sister's room to present her apology. When I later talked with her, she said: "I did not want to apologize. It would have been better if we did not talk to each other. But mother interfered, as usual, and I cannot make her angry."

Both men and women avoid provoking parental anger, by compliance if at all possible, and by deceit if necessary. Although modes of parent-child interaction have become more flexible over the years, people of the middle generation still maintain considerable social distance from their parents. They continue to observe traditional rituals of respect, such as standing up as one of them enters the room and kissing their hands in the morning. They also abstain from smoking in their presence, from excessive laughing, and from raising the voice above what is considered normal for ordinary conversation. Generally, distance is more strictly kept toward the father than toward the mother. Boys, especially, often ignore conventional restrictions in the presence of their mothers as they mature into manhood. They would, for example, smoke, not stand up for her, be relaxed in her company, and even show temper; but they continue to be more formal to their fathers. Daughters also relax more with their mothers than with their fathers, but they seldom ignore as many of the restrictions as their brothers do. Since a girl reaches "social" maturity not at puberty but at marriage and with the birth of a child (or when past marriage age), a daughter, compared to her brother, begins to voice her independence and even disagreement with her mother relatively late. The threat of her mother's *ghadab*, however, continues to operate in controlling her behavior. In several cases known to me a woman resorted to this sanction in pressuring her daughter to behave more "reasonably" toward her husband.

On the whole, the middle and younger generations show little difference in the ideals of parent-child relations. They state that the relationship should be one of loving care from mother, firm discipline and unlimited support from father, gratitude and obedience from the children. Ideally, the two parents are credited with equal rights to respect and support from all children—but there are grounds that favor a mother over the father, for as the Prophet said: "Your mother, then your mother, then your mother, and then your father," meaning that a mother deserves thrice the affection, gratitude, and respect due a father.

But in actual behavior a father, because of his long absence from the house and his expected firmness, is accorded more respect than the mother. The latter is viewed as a source of love and compassion within the household. She serves in childhood, nurses in sickness, and maneuvers to win her children a relative freedom of movement—as in outings for boys and girls—where the father may not grant it. The father has remained the source of discipline and ideally provides firmness to balance a mother's love.

Actually, however, this is really a consequence of a woman's character, and I know many cases where the children were disciplined by their mother rather than their father. Indeed, the father's long absence from the house removes him from the daily routine of the children's lives and maintains the distance which makes him the source of firmness and the parent with whom more social distance is observed. That is not to say that there are no cases where fathers encourage their children to become less formal with them and do not care to have their children observe the norms of respect—yet, these are valued as a "father different from all fathers, who does not shout or beat his children, does not deprive them [of the fulfillment of their desires]. Instead, he jokes and laughs; he kisses them and plays with them, and he would never have anyone anger them."

In reality, as I have observed, the middle- and younger-generation women do not conform to the behavior patterns of the older generation. Though many of them restrain themselves from giving their parents a rude answer and though they do not defy their parents' orders, they have begun to set limits on their parents' involvement in their lives. A middle-generation woman who was firmly reproached by her father (because she quarreled with her husband) said to her friends in the absence of her parents: "It's a bit too much. He is my father, and his *rida* is a duty which I have to observe. But this is my private life. If he does not want me to anger him, he must not interfere between my husband and me. I don't want to submit to my husband simply so as not to anger my father."

Middle- and younger-generation women often differ with their mothers, raise their voices in the course of discussions, and even ignore some of their orders. However, the violation of some norms of respect and the nonobservance of others is not a source of conflict, since the parents themselves are less demanding in these respects than the parents of the older generation. As one old woman explained to me: "Things are different now—in the past, we could not contradict our parents. We couldn't do anything without their permission. We feared and respected them. Today, young girls might even cross the room with shoes while their mothers are sitting down on the floor [a sign of disrespect]. They smoke in front of their mothers, some of them might even discuss love and sex with their mothers. Didn't I tell you that those who have shame are dead?"

Fathers, too, are now treated with comparatively less formality than in former generations, but with considerably more respect than mothers. I have observed many girls joke with their middle-generation parents, question their decisions at times (such as when they are not granted permission to go out); but I have never seen them, for example, smoke in a father's presence or remain in a reclining position if he enters the room. Though children may question a father's order, they dare neither to ignore nor to defy it.

Role Conflict of Married Women

The married daughter is caught between two people whose authority she must accept. As an unmarried woman, her movements outside the house were determined by her father; it was his desires that were respected and carried out. When she marries, she should obey her husband. Indeed, the Islamic view, as defined and interpreted by men and women in the society, equates obedience to a husband with obedience to Allah and comes, ideally, before obedience to a father. Yet, this cannot be put so categorically, since it may be the case in fact that a woman will take her father's advice at the expense of conflict with her husband.

The married woman thus must cope with possible conflict between the two most important men in her life. On the one hand, she must obey her father, achieve his *rida,* and not bring about his *ghadab.* Observation of the expected brings reward from Allah and recognition from the community, just as a violation of the expected brings punishment by Allah, both in this world and in the next, as well as criticism from the community. On the other hand, she must obey her husband and observe his wishes. This, too, is a religious duty that is backed by the value system of the community. To men in both roles the woman's position is almost the same: they are her supporters and protectors, and they are also the ultimate source of decisions affecting her behavior. Clearly, when the experiences of the two men are so different as to result in differing values and outlooks on life, their decisions can create potentially conflict-ridden situations.

The conditions of rapid change after the discovery of oil in the peninsula and the resultant exposure to different societies and cultures, as well as the increasing resort to education, has made the experience of younger-generation men qualitatively different from that of their parents. As young boys, they were sent abroad for formal schooling; they lived temporarily in Egypt and Lebanon and followed this by frequent trips to Europe. It is not surprising, then, that they have modified the older generation's views on several scores, many of which relate to women: middle-generation men have a less strict view of the veil, and they now readily accept and encourage the education of girls—a matter borne out by the fact that formal schooling for girls did not begin until the daughters of the women of the middle generation came of age.

In the realm of wife-husband relationships, middle-generation couples show less specialization of roles, which begin to overlap in several respects. It cannot be claimed that for middle-generation couples there is what Bott called "joint roles,"[10] but rather the roles become less separate so that a father participates more actively in the socialization of his daughter, the wife more in that of her son, and the two spouses coordinate decisions affecting their children. These trends are considerably clearer with younger-generation couples, with whom the separation of roles, though present, is considerably less pronounced than that of older-generation couples.

The difference in values held by the older generation from those of the middle and younger generations makes it fairly common for a girl to be married to a man whose views on, for example, veiling, girl's education, and marriage differ from those of her father. Though ideally she is to conform to her husband's ideas, obedience and loyalty to her father are social values which cannot be ignored. As an old woman explained to me:

> No one is like one's family [agnatic group]—no one can compare with a father. Even a husband cannot be compared to the father. A husband may love a woman and do for her everything he can, but a woman would be foolish to listen to him at the expense of her father's satisfaction with her. After all, her life with her husband is at the mercy of one word [i.e., divorce]. If he says it, she is thrown out. Whom has she got? Her father. No matter how much anger, no matter what disagreeable things can happen between them, his house is her house; he is responsible for her by the *shari'ah* [legal code], and he can never let her down. That is why a wise woman satisfies her husband and never angers her father.

As this statement shows, women may ignore the cultural ideal of obedience to husband to follow another: obedience to father. The behavior of middle- and younger-generation women in doing so reflects their recognition of their precarious status as wives; they attempt to maximize the benefits from the role which offers them more security. This is usually the role of daughter. Hence, in most cases, a wise woman does not allow the conflict to get out of hand and so anger her father that they cease to exchange visits. The following two cases illustrate this situation.

> Rajyah married her patrilateral parallel cousin, who went to school in Jiddah but often traveled to other Middle Eastern countries and Europe. When they married thirty years ago, he took her out with him for a drive in the car. She was fully veiled. As they came to an isolated area, he asked her to unveil her face, as there was no one around. It was her bad luck that a friend of her father passed and recognized them. Upon hearing the story, her father was very angry and had a fight with her. She pointed out that it was her husband who suggested it to her, to which her father replied: "If you unveil your face in public, I shall forever be angry [*ghadaban*] with you and shall

never forgive you. I shall never enter your house and you'll never set foot in mine if this is repeated." Rajyah explained to me that throughout the first ten years or so of her marriage she did not unveil in Egypt when her father was present, and she certainly did not do so in Saudi Arabia. "Though my husband often told me to remove the veil in Cairo, I took it around with me when father came to Cairo, because I did not want him to be angry with me."

In the other case, a middle-generation man allowed his daughter's groom to visit the house and see his bride before the wedding ceremony, after concluding the marriage document. Such practice was new in Jiddah, where until the last twenty-five years first visual contact was on the wedding night. Understandably, the man's father-in-law was considerably alarmed by what he heard. He came to his daughter's house and reprimanded her and her husband for what they had done "to their daughter." The man said to his daughter: "You have always been obedient to me. I shall decrease [or withhold] my *rida* from you if you permit such things to happen again." Following this, the groom was not permitted to visit his bride again until the wedding night.

Despite the choice, in these two cases, to accept the father's position, the result is not always thus with middle- and younger-generation couples. It is important to focus on these conflicts involving fathers, daughters, and husbands for the light they shed on the nature of obedience.

The first case above occurred when the couple was temporarily residing with the wife's father until such time as they could build their own residence. Since the husband's father was deceased, there was no question of viripatrilocal residence. No less important is the fact that the financial resources of the husband were modest, and he was, in fact, receiving occasional loans to purchase land and build his home from his father-in-law.

More recently, this same woman faced another conflict between husband and father in which the circumstances were quite different:

Rajyah's father fell seriously ill and required hospitalization, followed by a long period of convalescence. She and her husband—by then married over twenty-five years—were living abroad. Rajyah flew in to take care of her father, but after a couple of weeks she began to express her desire to return to her husband. Discussing her priorities with me she said: "I know my father is sick. But what can I do? I have a husband to look after who needs me beside him. I trust that others will look after my father, but I have to be with my husband."

This case sums up changes in the wider society. It is important that by the time of the second incident, Rajyah's father, previously a leading figure in Jiddah society, had been weakened by sickness and loss of considerable wealth. Also, Rajyah's husband had become immensely rich over the years. Another important factor is the long duration of Rajyah's marriage, one untroubled by divorce. This created greater security for her in her role as wife. All these factors explain the outcome of the case and indirectly throw light on the nature of obedience itself.

What, then, do these cases suggest? An important constituent element of obedience is economic dependence, whether on father or on husband. Though clearly the conflict arises when the woman leaves her natal family, the financial resources of husband vis-à-vis father are relevant for the young couple's perception of their autonomy from him. The same considerations temper the father's stance in this conflict, for if the disagreement were to polarize around husband's and father's demands, conflict might bring divorce and a return of the daughter to her natal home. There, she reverts to being the financial responsibility of her father. The potential conflict is further reduced by any beneficial economic ties that may obtain between the woman's father and his affines—i.e., the family of her husband. Divorce would throw these ties into doubt but not annul them.

Economic dependence is a significant factor in the obedience of the wife to the husband, but it is not the only factor. Women have often opted for the relative autonomy they gain from their status as married women living in neolocal households, away from the authority of their husbands' fathers. This factor becomes even more important when long years of marriage and the birth of children bring security to the status of wife and make divorce more unlikely. When women obey husbands rather than fathers, this should be understood in terms of the growing importance of the conjugal bond in the ideology of the domestic groups.

Of course, the security and support inherent in the father-daughter relationship is sometimes manipulated by married women against their husbands in that a wife may threaten to return to her natal household, or, if her father is deceased, to the house of her brother. The effectiveness of this threat depends on the existence of the father and on his status in the society, together with his possible blood relationship to his daughter's husband. When the bride's father is alive and enjoys a prestigious status in the community, the husband's behavior is somewhat checked by the consequences that a divorce may have on his relationship to his *arham*. This check becomes more effective when the wife's father is also an agnatic kinsman. Indeed, marriages between *ahl*—more than those involving male friends—may somewhat reduce the conflict in which a married woman is caught, as the husband himself must, to an extent, respect the opinion of his father's brother, or his mother's brother.

If the conflict leads to divorce, the woman can find refuge in her father's home. As a divorcée there, she acquires greater freedom of movement without referring to her father except on occasions of long absence from the house. But her status as a divorcée minimizes her chances for a second marriage, especially when she has children, whom she usually brings to her father's house if they are young enough to be in her custody (by *shari'ah* law boys are in the custody of the mother until age seven or nine, and girls until they come of age; a mother's remarriage forfeits these rights). Furthermore, she is at a disadvantage because a husband, with whom one has a chance to construct a relationship of intimacy, is for that very reason easier to manipulate to fulfill personal interests than a father. Divorce, therefore, while it does not leave a woman without recourse, carries its penalties.

Although easy divorce is theoretically possible, it is not common among these families. For example, in the sample there were five cases of divorce in all the three generations. Conditional, not terminal divorce, is not infrequent, especially with older-generation couples, and it was mostly used to control the woman's behavior rather than to dissolve the marriage bond. Nevertheless, most women express a fear of divorce as an alternative open to men but denied to women. Perhaps this unrealistic fear of divorce is perpetuated as a fiction to guarantee the asymmetric power relationship between husband and wife. Among most women of all three generations the stability of married life is seen to be dependent on the will of the husband. Consequently, the husband-wife relationship is potentially precarious and cannot be a source of security in any final sense to a woman.

In more positive terms, women seek to achieve the *rida* of their father and of their husbands. The *rida* of both is perceived to be the *rida* of Allah. Such fusion of moral precepts and Islamic dogma is salient in Jiddah society. Appropriate behavior, i.e., socially approved behavior, is, ideally, religiously virtuous or righteous behavior. Thus, the values governing husband-wife and parent-child relationships are also Islamic injunctions. More generally speaking, the Qur'anic ideal of righteous conduct comes very close to the ideals for appropriate behavior expressed and, to a considerable degree also observed, by men and women in the Jiddah families.

Role Changes

The set of roles described above undergoes considerable change when the head of the household dies. Informants say: "All death breaks the heart, but the death of a household head is the worst. It closes down a house and may disband a family." This sums up the dramatic changes which the death of a breadwinner brings to the lives of his women dependents. Following the initial shock in which the realities of death unfold upon the living, and the grief resulting from the loss of a beloved one, the first problem which women face is maintenance. In this society women without husbands cannot live alone (except possibly widows) unless they have no living male kin. The process of adapting to the new situation results in a redefinition of roles between members of the household.

When a household head dies leaving minor children, some close male agnatic kin of the deceased (for example, a brother) becomes responsible for them and supervises their inherited property. This can sometimes include the widow's share as well. Where no such male kin exist, or where conflict exists (either between the deceased and his agnatic kin, or between the deceased's children and/or his wife and the deceased's other relatives), the responsibility may be delegated to the widow's brother. When sons are mature, they either individually or cooperatively shoulder the responsibility for their deceased father's household, which includes the deceased's wife and all unmarried and divorced daughters. In the event that the deceased leaves more than one son, some of whom have married and moved out while others are unmarried and still resided with the father, the responsibility falls upon the eldest single son if he has completed his education and has a regular income. If, on the other hand, the single sons are still not at that stage of life, the household becomes the responsibility of the eldest married son, who, according to his financial means, either merges it with his household or retains two separate households. Where there are considerable differences in the financial means of the sons, the most affluent takes the responsibility for his father's household. Since such arrangements are really dependent on the economic means of the sons, and since in the past the eldest son was often the wealthiest, he assumed the financial burden. However, recent economic changes associated with the oil enterprise have made it possible for sons to be wealthier than the fathers. With their education, sons were no longer restricted to their father's business, and some chose other careers, with the result that the eldest brother may no longer be the wealthiest.

The pattern for assuming financial responsibility for a father's household has changed accordingly. In some cases this role is still assumed by the eldest son. There are also cases where sons cooperate in providing the budget for their father's household, and cases where a son other than the eldest shoulders the responsibility alone.

Women have property, since they inherit and own valuables such as jewelry, as already noted. This economic independence is reduced by the norms restricting a woman from living alone. There are no cases where single women of these families live alone. Some widows do so only if they have children, especially sons. The one case where a divorced woman lived in an independent household with her nine-year-old son, subsequent to her father's death, elicited cruel criticism and gossip.

Ideally, women dependents of the deceased can select the son with whom they wish to live. They base their decisions on compatibility of character, as well as on their relations with the son's wife. If there are unmarried sons, women usually elect to live with one of them, for this eliminates chances of conflict with a daughter-in-law. However, they can do so only if such sons are able to support them or if any wealthier sons agree to provide the budget for this independent household. If the deceased's wife is alive, widowed, unmarried, and divorced daughters sometimes live with their mother if a son is willing to provide for all of them.

By assuming the financial responsibility, the son also assumes the role of a household head, with the rights and duties described above. The women dependents of his late father become his own, and although they may have their own financial means, they may spend it on those luxuries which the son's budget cannot meet. Indeed, the ideal brother is one who saves his unmarried sister's money until he "transfers" her to a husband. Like her father, he would provide for her trousseau and pay for the wedding ceremony. Concomitantly, he assumes his father's authority vis-à-vis the women of the household. From him they must obtain permission for their movements outside the house and the city; and his decisions regarding their attire and behavior must be observed.

The relationship between mother and son is in practice redefined to meet this change in authority. On the ideal level the authority of the son must be tempered by his duties as a son not to anger his mother and to observe her wishes to secure her *rida*. Similarly, the mother's authority to inflict *ghadab* is restrained by the realities of her dependence on her son. In practice, however, this redefinition of roles means that she can dispute his orders but must accede to his wishes, for "He is now the man of the house, and we have no one other than him, after Allah."

The new situation increases the potential for conflict between husband's mother and son's wife, especially in the event that the son's budget can support only one household and the two separate households are merged. For the young wife this means a sacrifice of a measure of independence gained in her conjugal household—a fact which is aggravated by the differences in experience and values held by the older- and younger-generation women. The relationship between husband's mother and son's wife is further strained, as the widow loses the financial independence which her husband's household guaranteed and now becomes dependent upon the son, whose wife might object to the expenditure involved.

The unmarried daughter experiences similar changes in rights and duties. As I described above, the daughter's rights to maintenance, care, clothing, and education were secured by her father and backed by the *shari'ah* law. Although by custom her brother, assuming the late father's role, provides for as many of these needs as is possible or as he sees fit to do, it remains understood that if it is not volunteered it can be secured by law. In return she observes his orders and extends to him the obedience she extended to her father, even when the brother is younger. This obedience she must extend to all her brothers, with priority to the one with whom she lives.

This new situation often involves a curtailment of such freedom of mobility as was gained through the cultural ideal of parent-daughter love which she could maneuver to meet her interests. However, by the same token, the presence of a mother often improves conditions for the unmarried girl. Indeed, as the case below will show, a widow may maneuver her rights of obedience from her son to gain more freedom for her unmarried daughter:

When Maha's father died, she and her mother lived with her oldest brother, Rajab, who was a middle-generation married man. Being very strict, Rajab seldom allowed the women in his house to go out on social visits. Maha, however, had many friends, and she often managed to visit them. Sometimes, her mother got her the permission to go out. At other times, when Rajab was obstinate and Maha adamant, the mother allowed her to go out and covered up for her absence. One day, Rajab discovered that Maha had gone out without his permission. When he returned home, he asked to see her. The mother, knowing the fury that would break loose on Maha, decided to meet him instead of her. When Rajab threatened a conditional divorce of his wife if Maha went out again, her mother retorted: "And if you do that, she and I will leave this house, even if we take shelter in the slums, and my heart shall forever remain angry with you." Fearing the consequences of his action, Rajab dismissed the incident, and Maha resumed her outings after a reasonable lapse of time.

While such threats are tolerated from a mother, rebellion of an unmarried sister against her brother brings bitter criticism from the community. Similarly, within the house the unmarried daughter's authority changes. As an adult in her father's household, her authority was second only to that of her mother; in her new role as an unmarried sister, such authority becomes marginal to that of her brother's wife. As an old informant put it, "In your father's house you have the prerogative to express your likes and dislikes—as, for example, in running the house—but with a brother the house is that of his wife."

Following her father's death, an unmarried woman's consent to marriage was sought by the religious specialist who drew up the marriage contract (*ma'dhun shar'i*), even in the past when women were seldom consulted. However, the option to object is really contingent upon her brother's approval, for ideally he controls the final decision on his sister's marriage. In cases where more than one brother exists, a consensus of opinion is the ideal and is often sought. If it is not forthcoming, and if the objection from other brothers is not based on "good reasons," the brother with whom the sister resides can make the final decision.

In practice, the effort of a mother, or possibly married sisters, to help a single woman marry and thus obtain a measure of relative independence is sometimes greater than observance of a brother's opinion, even if he is financially responsible for his sister. However, it must be, and always is, their widowed mother who takes the initiative in pressuring the brother to consent to the marriage. Even if the girl is nearly past accepted marriage age, in no cases that I know of did she take the initiative herself, which would mean that she was rebelling against her brother. Women and men, especially of the older and middle generations, disapprove of either objecting to a marriage or actively seeking one and would criticize the woman for it bitterly. It is therefore only her mother, or married older sibling, who can exert pressure in her interest. The following case is an illustration:

Lulwa, a middle-generation woman, lived with her widowed mother in the house of her eldest brother, Nuri, who assumed responsibility for his late father's household. It was from Nuri that Lulwa had to obtain permission for her outings, and not from Hazim, her second-eldest brother. Hazim shared the house with them but not the budget, because it was Nuri, not Hazim, who was "responsible" for her. Her mother helped her a great deal. Women considered Lulwa's lot better than it would have been if her mother were dead. She often spoke out on Lulwa's behalf, even when Nuri was scolding Lulwa—a stance which Lulwa could not take vis-à-vis her older brother. When Lulwa went out without her brother's permission, her mother covered up for her, an act of love and support Lulwa would not have gotten from her brother's wife, for example. Lulwa had many suitors, but Nuri always turned them down, perhaps because he needed her continued service in raising his eldest daughter. Lulwa was nearly 35 years of age when her mother's half-brother's son asked to marry her. Nuri declined. Lulwa's mother, who wanted her daughter to have a life of her own, independent of her brother's wife, was firm in seizing what looked like Lulwa's last chance of marriage. She appealed to Lulwa's two married sisters for support: all, including Hazim, agreed that the proposal should be accepted. When Nuri did not change his mind, his mother quarreled with him and left with Lulwa to go to the house of her wealthy daughter. The mother and her two married daughters commissioned Hazim to communicate acceptance to the groom. Following that, the women set out preparing for the wedding. Faced with this united stand Nuri had to accede. But the conflict with his mother had to be resolved. Following an appeal from her brother, Lulwa's mother went to his house, where Hazim came to reconcile them. She agreed to return to his house after the wedding ceremony, which was held in Lulwa's sister's house.

The constraints which an unmarried woman faces upon her father's death are not the same for a divorced woman. By virtue of her divorcée status, she attains relative freedom of movement, so that she need obtain permission only for a long absence from the house. In regard to a second marriage, she cannot be forced against her will, but she must also seek her brother's consent.

Although the ideals of sister-brother relationships where the brother is household head have not changed for the younger generation, in practice the relationships are not what they were for older- and middle-generation women. Indeed, some younger-generation unmarried daughters have great mobility; they go out as often as they like and simply notify their mother. It is only for trips out of the city that they seek their brother's permission. Similarly, with them forced marriage is not a realistic possibility. I have no cases where the brothers objected to the marriage of their young, unmarried sisters. In view of the greater mobility a younger-generation woman has, it is reasonable to expect that the final marriage decision would be hers and that her brother, though objecting, would agree. This greater freedom, in comparison with older- and middle-generation women, is largely a result of the education and different experience of younger-generation men. Furthermore, the woman herself is now educated and sometimes even has a job. With these new assets, her freedom of movement and her control over decisions affecting her life are beginning to increase. The woman, in her steps toward some measure of autonomy, is faced not with an older-generation man but rather with young, educated men whose values have changed, allowing for less separation of women from men and indeed a relatively greater degree of autonomy.

A young boy, on the other hand, does not, and did not in the past, experience much change in his life after the death of his father. Because he is a minor, his older brothers make decisions affecting his education (for example, what school he should go to in what country), and they even discipline him, though usually only to keep the boy conforming to the norms which his father had established for the household. An adult whose father has died receives only counsel from his brothers, and he could, if he so desired, live alone. Men in the older generation had the authority of a father also in regard to his marriage; the younger brother often agreed to their choice out of respect and obedience. However, since all older-generation marriages were arranged, the groom seldom had reason to object to a brother's choice of a bride for him. Despite the ideal of obedience and respect to an older brother "who has brought you up," the older brother now only gives advice on marriage of his brother but cannot dictate his wishes to him. The following case illustrates the freedom men now have to select their partners while denying the same rights to a woman:

Even before his father's death, Iqbal took decisions regarding his three sister's movements. Because he was the eldest son, his father delegated to him most of his authority and in fact ordered his three middle-generation daughters to obey Iqbal even though he was younger. The daughters had many suitors, but they were always rejected because Iqbal and his father seldom agreed on their evaluations of the suitor. By the time their father died, the three sisters had nearly passed marriage age. Iqbal assumed financial responsibility for the household and continued his support of his younger brother, Talal, to complete his education. Being a "strict man," Iqbal often refused his sisters permission to go out, and they had no alternative but to obey. Some suitors came for the youngest of the three sisters, but Iqbal declined. Having no mother or siblings to back her, she could not influence Iqbal's decisions. Talal, on the other hand, returned home with a German wife. Commenting on the women's lot, an old woman said: "You see, the girl must obey her brother. If she rebels against him, people will slash her with their tongues. For a man it is different. Talal married a Christian. Of course, Iqbal did not like that, but he could not tell him anything. The unmarried sisters, on the other hand—though older than he—are ruled by him. They cannot go out of the house without his permission. They are old, but they must comply, for what alternative have they got?"

When a wife dies, the implications are grave for her children but not necessarily for the household as a whole. Particularly alarming is the realistic fear that the father will take a second wife who will not be a surrogate mother for the children. They will thus be deprived of the source of love and tenderness particularly associated with the role of mother. Although the father is expected to be loving to his children, this affection is very much tied to the presence of their mother. The mother is seen as mediating the father's authority and maneuvering to provide for her children's desires if they do not meet with the father's total approval. Thus women remind their children when the need arises that they have endured a hard marriage to spare them the oppressive treatment of a stepmother. Despite the cultural ideal for a father to provide for his children's needs and wants, women see the practice of this ideal to be contingent upon the presence of their mother. Thus, for example, a middle-generation woman who had a quarrel with her sick daughter reminded her, "All the expenses for your treatment, all these trips we have to take to Europe for your sake are paid for by your father. By Allah, had it not been for me your father would not have done all this!"

The death of a wife does not lead to a restructuring of roles within the household except in the relationship between children and father and children and father's wife. The father continues to be the head of the household, and it is acceptable, indeed expected, for him to take a new wife to manage his household, look after him and the children.

The father still continues his obligation to his dependent children after he takes a new wife and is expected to be "fair and just" in dealing with them and their half siblings. Partial treatment of siblings, especially of half siblings, is criticized and regarded as an act that will bring punishment from Allah. In reality, fathers attempt to realize this ideal, but variations occur, depending on the character of the man and of his wife.

It is the eldest unmarried daughter who must adjust most to the loss of a mother, as she assumes her deceased mother's role in running the household and socializing her younger siblings. In this role her relationship to her brothers does not change, as it is the father who supervises them, unless they are children who spend most of their time in the household. He may, however, consult with an older daughter about schools, careers, and certainly marriage for her brothers.

To her younger sisters the older daughter now assumes the discipline and responsibility of a mother, even in the presence of the father's wife. Daughters both young and old theoretically have to submit to the authority of their father's wife in managing the household and in controlling their outings.

Clearly then, the death of a breadwinner is of great basic consequence for the household. The adjustments and redefinition of roles within the nuclear family shifts authority from father to son; the financial dependence of mother on son effectively makes filial obedience secondary to male dominance.

The death of a household head also leads to the distribution of inheritance among the nuclear family. Since most families studied have their wealth in shares in companies or in real estate, distribution of inheritance is a complex process that may extend for years. The problem is further complicated by the necessity of securing the consensus of beneficiaries before any step in the distribution can be put into effect. For example, all heirs must agree before a house in the estate can be sold. If one member disagrees, he or she has grounds to block the transaction. In consequence, the distribution of inheritance is much delayed, since the property itself must be converted into liquid assets. Delegation of proxy (*tawkil*) to one of the legatees reduces these problems, and it has become common practice.

Two cultural ideals help to reduce the adverse consequences generated by the realities of the inheritance system. First, the cultural ideal to shun discussion of inheritance matters, except with those in whom one has confidence, helps to prevent public knowledge of disagreements. Furthermore, a family which is known to have discussed inheritance problems—even among themselves—before a "reasonable" lapse of time following death is criticized in these terms: "They could not wait for the poor man to die. This is '*ayb*. They have no shame! How could they have the heart to discuss such matters when their mouths are full of blood [i.e., when death is still recent]." Second, the cultural ideal to value sibling and kinship ties above material gain helps to restrain polarizing conflict among heirs. Heirs are often encouraged to compromise because of their kinship ties and also because conflict over inheritance, if known to the community, is considered "scandalous" and has an adverse effect on the reputation of the family.

In reality, however, cultural ideals do not curb the material interests of the heirs, and often siblings discuss inheritance and may even have conflicts over it. For those who do not compromise another alternative to public scandal is resort to their older male *ahl*, *arham*, and even close friends to settle their differences. Above their kinship ties to the heirs, these mediators must have a reputation for "wisdom" and fairness. These qualities are felt to be so important in a mediator that they are sought even where kinship ties do not exist. Although the decisions of these men are not legally binding, the respect which the young accord them, plus the negative value placed on resort to the courts for resolving family differences, often leads to successful mediation.

Jasim, who was a blind man, married his father's brother's daughter. They had two sons, and then his wife died. He asked to marry his late wife's sister, Lina. He waited until he got his two sons married, and then he married Lina. They had one daughter. His married sons lived with him. When Jasim died, the power of proxy was given by all heirs to Jasim's eldest son, Walid. The household remained as it was in the past, with Walid as its head. He arranged for his half-sister's marriage and paid for her trousseau and wedding ceremony from her share of the inheritance. Lina continued to live in Walid's household. She often went on trips to Egypt and took money from him. He kept a record of her expenses, and one day he told her that she had exhausted all her share of the inheritance. Knowing the wealth of her late husband, Lina suspected that this information was not true. In exasperation, she left Walid's house and went to live with her brother. She did not want to resort to court action, for after all, "Walid is my sister's son. Besides, we cannot drag the family's name into the mud by taking the dispute to court." So Lina decided to find a mediator. She could not appeal to her brother to prevail on Walid, for despite their kinship ties she knew that her brother could not influence Walid. Lina said, "I needed some men Walid would be too ashamed to turn down. So I went to Najwah, my good friend. Her father, Bani, is a re-spectable man from the best of families in the city. Besides, he used to be a good friend of my late husband." She asked Najwah to explain her case to him and to ask him to settle the matter with Walid. Bani accepted, and a few days later he went with Jamil, another good friend of her husband and also an eminent man in the society, to discuss the matter with Walid. They were finally able to get her S.R. 90,000 (about $25,000) from him. Lina continued: "You see, Walid could not turn down such respectable men. If he did, everybody would have put him in the wrong. Had it not been for those men, I wouldn't have had a thing from Walid. Since then, I have often prayed to Allah to bless them and reward them on my behalf."

Although most of the cases that informants could remember had either been settled quietly without dispute or through mediation, when disputes did occur, they could drag on a long time. In one case, the dispute was actually taken to court ten years ago. While the family involved was, and still is, considered "of the good families," the man who went to court is described as "foolish, irresponsible, and with no head for the good word of respectable people."

For women inheritance does not bring the financial security it brings to men because their restriction to the "world inside the house" precludes their actual control of their property. Lacking the knowhow to invest in business, women always delegate authority to manage their property to men. Ideally, a woman can delegate this authority to any man of her choice, but an unmarried woman always delegates it to her eldest brother. A married woman has the alternative of delegating it to her husband.

Although giving a proxy to the husband is accepted, it is preferable to keep him out of sibling squabbles. In two cases involving older- and middle-generation couples the wives wanted their husbands to be their *wakil* (deputy), but in both cases the husbands declined, maintaining that their wives' brothers were the "right" people to have the proxy, and that, as husbands, they should not be made parties to disagreements between brothers and sisters.

Whether a woman chooses a brother or a husband as a *wakil*, she has little control over her property and is always dependent on a man to administer it for her according to his best judgment. That judgment is seldom questioned by older-generation or most middle-generation women, since they know little about business matters. Questioning any decision is *'ayb*, since it implies doubt of the man's honesty. Even where women have reason for grievances, they consider it *'ayb* to complain to others and thus expose men with whom they share kinship ties to criticism. The following case is an illustration:

> Hazim died, leaving two married daughters and one married son. The women, not wanting to drag their husbands into the matters of family property, made their brother a *wakil* to administer the property. By the time of fieldwork six years had passed since Hazim's death. Until then, neither of these two older-generation women knew how much they had inherited

from their father, nor did they feel that they could discuss the matter with their brother. One of them explained, "He gives us money whenever we need it. How could we offend him by discussing these matters with him? It would be 'ayb to do that."

There is a noticeable change with some middle- and younger-generation women, who now feel that "there is no 'ayb in knowing what Allah has made their right." Redefining the concept of 'ayb, some of these women now require detailed information of their share in the inheritance and an account of its management. Such knowledge, of course, is a condition of control of property, which is likely to give women a power base.

Conclusions

As can be seen from the foregoing, a dense network of roles adopted by men, women, and children exists in the family life of the *ahl al-balad* elite. These roles have been subject to pressure as a result of overall change in the environment and people's perception of new opportunities for modifying the old community norms governing male-female and parent-child relations.

No structural change in these relations has taken place, however. Segregation and asymmetry continue to be the principal elements of male-female relations. Thus, evasion of a husband's orders prohibiting unveiling is out of the question. But modifications in the essential structure of male-female relations may be seen in a woman's ability to circumvent her husband's wishes in the matter of outings.

Middle- and younger-generation women have increasingly established their right to go out without specific permission in individual cases. Instead, they will make general declarations of intention to their husbands, who are expected to be tolerant of this more relaxed approach. If the husband is adamant against her going in a particular case, the matter may still not be over, since even in this case there are other strategies available to women before they exhaust their repertoire of responses. For example, as we have seen, women may seek the intercession of other family members, such as their daughters, to plead their case.

The ideology of these domestic groups slowly changes in consequence of changes in men-women relationships. And the latter, in turn, become altered as a result of external factors, such as increasing education, travel abroad, the influx of foreigners due to the oil boom, and the like. Of course, it is important to note that ideology can shape social relations, as well. For example, the ideology of domestic groups worked effectively to maintain hierarchical differentiation between men and women, on the one hand, and old and young on the other.

Active renegotiating of their privileges has led women to establish the following rights: (1) to spend the household budget; (2) to participate in decision-making over the children's futures; (3) to participate in joint visits with their husbands to mixed gatherings; (4) as daughters, to challenge their mothers by ignoring the latter's wishes on certain issues, as long as this does not involve incurring their mother's *ghadab*; (5) as legatees of wills, having the right to clarify the nature of their inheritance, rather than rely on the good will of men.

Such strategies become intelligible not by reference to the norms alone but to people's interpretation of these norms in the light of their own interests. As might be expected, the strategies have been limited by the working of the sets of key concepts, *'ayb/dhanb* and *ghadab/rida*. These concepts are sanctions on behavior which, because they apply over a wide range of situations, are variously interpreted. People have the latitude to turn them around and stress different nuances of meaning to accord with their perceived advantage.

Both sets of concepts reflect, on the ideological level, the fusion in Jiddah society of religious dogma and social norms. This fusion has not, however, been a static one. What is *'ayb* behavior changes, and what incurs *ghadab* is redefined. New realities throw into relief contradictions on the ideological level between sacred and secular concepts (as in property rights for women) and lead to a realigning of the latter in terms of the former. New realities also highlight disparities between reality and the ideology, as in the case of young men negotiating dissent without risking the *ghadab* of parents.

In any case, the chances for expanding their autonomy are increasing for these women, especially for the younger generation. This could well have a sustained effect on the patterns of power distribution between men and women in the society.

NOTES

1. Dwyer, *Images and Self-Images*, p. 67.
2. *Ibid.*, p. 101.
3. See Ortner, "Is Female to Male?"
4. *Ibid.*, pp. 72, 73.
5. See Hurgronje, *Mekka*, passim.
6. Under Islamic law, a single utterance of the divorce formula is revocable; only a triple pronouncement or the third of three separate pronouncements terminates the marriage.
7. I was unable to gather data on the impact of nannies in the socialization of children. The reasons for this are varied. Nannies of the older- and middle-generation women were always slaves who combined housework with child care. They came mostly from Yemen, African countries, and occasionally from tribal groups in the peninsula. Hurgronje, in *Mekka*, pp. 106–7, gives a detailed description of such slaves and their role in Maccan society as concubines, as domestic servants, and as nannies.

When, in 1963, slavery was abolished, the old slave women continued to live with the families. By the time of fieldwork, they were either dead or too old. The young slave women usually got married and left. They continued, however, to visit the families they served and often received annual donations from the religious tax, or *zakat*. Nannies for children of the younger generation are usually hired maids from the Seychelle Islands, Eritrea, Ethiopia, and, more recently, the Philippines or Sri Lanka. Since their Arabic is usually poor, conversation with the children is limited. Also, their contracts are usually for two years, and more often than not they are replaced by different people. Thus, there is no continuity in this interaction with children. However, foreign nannies are currently the object of intense public debate, and the subject of some research by women students in the universities. Foreign nannies are now portrayed by male journalists as a potential threat to local traditions, and more concern is expressed that Saudi women minimize such foreign intrusions into their families.

8. The *hadith* "Each of you is a shepherd and each shepherd is responsible to his flock" is behind this point of view.
9. Regarding this fear of exposure to "men's eyes," one is reminded of Mernissi's incisive observation that, according to Imam al-Ghazali (d. 1111), a Muslim philosopher, scholar, and Sufi, "the eye is undoubtedly an erog-

enous zone in the Muslim structure of reality. It is, accordingly, as able to give pleasure as the penis. A man can do as much damage to a woman's honor with his eyes as if he were to seize hold of her with his hands." Mernissi, *Beyond the Veil*, p. 83.

10. Elizabeth Bott, *Family and Social Networks*, p. 53.

CHAPTER FOUR

THE SOCIAL WORLD OF WOMEN: KINSHIP AND FRIENDSHIP

IN THESE FAMILIES separation of the sexes leads to the radical seclusion of women from public life. This segregation finds its cultural compensation in the elaboration of formal and informal networks of friendship and kin. Social visits are the major means for women to reduce their isolation. It is thus not surprising that they are more elaborate among women and are taken more seriously by them than by men. It will be seen, though, that while such visits are important for all three generations, younger-generation women's visiting networks are less extensive. The reason, as will be shown, is their increasing preference for giving priority to the conjugal relation.

In a society where women's mobility is restricted, social visits are the main channels of contact with other households and the community at large, in that they provide women with occasions to learn about current events, discuss new fashions in apparel and behavior, meet new people, form new ties of friendship, and sustain relationships from which support can be solicited. They also provide opportunities for women to select marriage partners for their relatives and friends.

Visiting patterns of men differ from those of women and, except for a recent development among middle- and younger-generation couples who may occasionally visit their friends and kinsmen jointly, the sexes perform these visits separately. On the whole, the men's visiting patterns on general occasions are simpler. They do not depend on absolute reciprocity—as do women's visits—but are meant to further business connections and careers.

Marriage, the naming of children, death, and sickness are occasions which call for visits among men and women alike. But in the case of men, on all occasions but death, a failure to make a visit is excusable except for close friends and kin.

Most middle- and younger-generation men in these families participate in male social gatherings composed of groups of friends and kinsmen who gather daily at the house of a common friend.[1] Some of these gatherings begin late in the afternoon and end with performance of the evening prayers; others begin shortly after sunset prayer and extend long after evening prayer. In these circles, coffee, tea, and perhaps dinner is served, and card playing is a common form of entertainment. Such gatherings usually take place in the homes of the wealthier men and those with influential connections in government administration and in business. Owing to these individuals' status in the community, their homes would appear to be the natural settings for these affairs.

In the world of women, friendship ties play a more important role as they come to constitute a network of support second only to kinship ties and at times equal to them. Thus, people have a special term, *wafa'*, that subsumes ties which they forge in extending their social world beyond the limits of the household. *Wafa'* refers to the pattern of social visits among women and the resultant ties of mutual support and assistance. It also refers to the reciprocal gifts and favors that cement these relationships.

For women social visits are the only means by which they can develop and sustain relationships with friends and kinswomen who can be called upon in hours of need for help and cooperation. Such ties are more important for women since they offer a source of security needed because of their relatively precarious status in society. The frequency of reciprocal visits indicates the degree of friendship and the concomitant commitment to mutual help between the two parties—be they kinswomen or friends.

Social visits are essential on occasions of death, grave sickness, and other crises if the relationship is to be maintained. They are preferred on occasions of marriage, birth, and naming if the relationship is to solidify. The principle of reciprocity underlies all kinds of social visiting, especially in the initial stage of a friendship and for the purpose of strengthening kinship ties. Similarly, visiting patterns can be reduced to terminate obligations that have become cumbersome.

Since friendship is a source of suport, failing to visit someone in a situation of crisis such as a death in the family results in a complete severing of relations. Not to visit on festive occasions, such as a marriage or a child's naming ceremony, affect the level of gift exchange but does not normally suspend relations. When a new family is established by marriage, relatives and friends of the bride and the groom and the wives of the groom's friends and relatives seize the opportunity to establish a new friendship with the bride. The bride then returns visits to all those whose friendship she chooses to maintain. Those whom she encourages and with whom she allows a development of interaction into at least a "formal friendship" have to visit her again at childbirth. If, by then, the degree of reciprocity is extended to include an exchange of gifts, naming is the next occasion on which a visit is essential.

Social visits are either formal or informal. When they are formal they are arranged by appointment among several friends of the hostess. Such visits, called *wu'ud,* make it possible for the hostess to entertain all those who "owe" her a visit at the same time. Because these visits include formal friends, with whom a degree of social distance is observed, the visits are highly ritualized: all those present dress up for the occasion, guests are received in the best room in the house, and refreshments are presented in conformity to a formal pattern. Formal visits always take place in the late afternoon or just after sunset prayer, and rarely extend into dinner parties unless this is announced in advance.

As explained earlier, until thirty years ago only married women participated in such visits; single girls were not exposed except to close friends and kinswomen. In the formal visits women would pick up information on girls of marriageable age and arrange to see them at a later point by dropping in on short notice, or by accompanying a mutual close friend to their homes in informal gatherings where single girls would be present. Increasingly, however, unmarried girls are taking part in formal gatherings held in their own homes or those of *ahl, arham,* and possibly close friends of the mother.

In a society that only since the 1970s began to tolerate visual contact between potential marriage partners, formal visits provide opportunities for women to see and examine the unmarried women in the host family and carry back descriptions to potential marriage partners.

During formal visits as well as on other visiting occasions, *ahl* and *arham* are expected. Since it is not possible to maintain the same degree of exchange with all such women, compatibility of character and closeness of residence influence one's choice of preferred partners. They are informed in advance, and the selection, to an extent, reflects the range of kin with whom greater frequency of social interaction is maintained, with the reciprocal commitment of support that such interaction entails. This is especially true as the absence of any relative known to be "close" to the hostess is brought up by the guests, who expect an explanation from the hostess. Lack of "reasonable" explanation is interpreted by the guests as a strain in the relationship with the absent individual.

In these visits and others (such as at death, naming, and marriage) the solidarity of the women's kin group is acted out before the community. The women relatives help attend to guests, clean and arrange whatever has escaped the attention of servants, and help the hostess keep the glittering, spotless, generous house valued by the community. Such roles are strictly reserved for relatives and close friends bound together by commitments, obligations of support, and old friendship.

Apart from death in the family, another occasion to receive guests is sickness. The number of visiting friends depends on the seriousness of the illness. Where it is a slight case of flu and other light ailments, only close friends are expected. Strained relations between close friends may excuse failure to pay visits for minor illness, but they must temporarily be forgotten in case of dangerous afflictions, and visits must be paid if the friendship is to be maintained. During such crises, visits are expected from formal friends, as well. Always, these visits are less ritualized than the formal ones. They take place in the mornings of Tuesdays and Thursdays. If paid on other days, or at other times of these days, such visits are said to be "heavy visits" that may prolong sickness. Most of the middle- and younger-generation women, however, take such views lightly and pay their visits any day, either in the morning or in the afternoon, depending on their free time.

Ahl and *arham* with whom a degree of interaction is maintained are either close or formal friends. People use the term *wufyan* to differentiate formal friends from *sudqan*, close friends. *Wufyan* also refers to *ajanib,* a term that means foreigners. With close friends, the level of formality is greatly reduced. They are received in any part of the house, are served whatever happens to be around, can move freely from one part of the house to another, and may even enter the kitchen. These women do not exchange visits on a one-to-one basis of reciprocity. As the frequency of visits increases, the household regards the guest friend as one of them and thus relaxes its formality and makes no special arrangements when she drops in for a visit.

But the hostess receives formal friends who have the same status or are wealthier than herself in the best salon in the house. She makes special arrangements to clean the guest area and to serve the guests. These guests restrict their movements to the room in which they are received. As the two parties exchange more and more visits, gifts, and favors, they become better friends, but the formality of the reception need not change. The room where the visit takes place then reflects the strength of the relationship between the two friends. There is no set number of visits exchanged before such barriers collapse—as an informant put it: "It depends on your character; if you are simple and humble and don't like to trouble people, then you volunteer to move into their living rooms." The initiative for this stage in the friendship always comes from the guest friend, as an offer by the hostess may be taken to communicate disrespect for the guest.

Once a person becomes a close friend, she becomes a partner in a process of support that extends from being a confidante in everyday affairs to playing special roles in the crisis situations of death, grave illness, and divorce, as well as on festive occasions of marriage and naming. The cooperation and empathy which one friend shows the other is secondary only to close kinship ties, and indeed, old friends are treated as if they were close kin. As I have argued elsewhere,[2] given this significance of friendship it is not surprising that women take a breach of expectations more seriously than men. They have subtle means of handling potential conflict when it threatens them and managing its consequences once it occurs.

Where formal friends (who are potential close friends) fail to do what is expected toward other formal friends, and the desire to continue the relationship exists, *'itab* is a means to this end. This term refers to a process whereby a disappointment is expressed without necessarily resorting to insults or show of anger that would only worsen the situation. The motive behind 'itab is clearly understood to be an earnest desire to resume good relations—as "criticism takes place because of [high] expectations." In all the cases I have observed, 'itab cleared the tension. During 'itab a friend communicates a message of disappointment to the friend who failed her and at the same time gives her the chance to apologize and reaffirm the friendship.

A party communicates 'itab personally over the telephone, for example, or during a formal visit at the house of a common friend. If the second party is eager to maintain the friendship, she presents an apology, followed by a quick correction of the lapse. For example, if the incident concerns the failure to pay a visit during sickness, the friend pays a visit soon after the confrontation and 'itab if she is interested in maintaining the relationship. Where she does not desire to do so, she dismisses the incident, ignores the promise given in the 'itab, and thereby "freezes" the relationship.

The same options are available when 'itab is communicated through a third party. Here, the offending party has the option of phoning to explain herself (as a result of the 'itab message she received) and by so doing preserve the friendship. She can also ignore the message and thereby widen the gulf between the two friends until the relationship ceases in the course of a further reduction in the expression of support.

'Itab is possible for all lapses except for a failure to present condolences—which always leads to a severing of relationships. This norm is strictly observed by women, and in all the cases I know failure to present condolences has, in fact, severed relations between the two parties.

In cases where a friendship is damaged not by direct confrontation but by gossip, a common friend may mediate between the women, communicating one friend's viewpoint to the other. Once this is done, the stage is set for reconciliation. The mediator arranges a meeting in her house or that of the older party when there is a considerable age difference. During such a meeting, 'itab takes place after the parties have shown their reconciliation by kissing one another.

Relations damaged because of direct confrontation during which "painful talk" occurred are not as easily mended. "Painful talk" refers to accusations of illicit sexual behavior, which, being a matter of greatest shame in the culture, rarely occurs. When such accusations are made, they result in the accused party's severing relations with her accuser for all events in life.[3] Only a major crisis, such as death in the family, provides the occasion when such severance can be remedied. In this situation a visit can be made without loss of face for the offending party.

Formal visits offer still another alternative to mend severed relations—but in contrast to the previous alternative the outcome is not guaranteed. If one party is adamant in not resuming the relationship, she abstains from the formal visit when she finds out from her hostess that the other party will be present. However, presence in the same formal visit is no guarantee of resumption of suspended relations. Both parties can use behavior patterns to indicate their options regarding the state of relations between them.

One of the two friends may opt to stand up as the second friend enters the room. Such behavior declares her intention to improve relations. Not standing up for an incoming friend would widen the gulf between them to the point of severing all relations. Ideally, the incoming friend has the option to salute, but actually she must do so because ignoring an outstretched hand is the highest insult and completely suspends relations, placing the insulting party in the wrong, even if the case were reversed prior to the incident. Only a neglect of condolence and matters of greater shame, that is, "painful talk" affecting honor, can justify such behavior to other women present.

In reality, the condition of "severed relations" need not be permanent between kinsfolk or even friends; relations are resumed when either party wants to do so. Unlike reconciliation, which "thaws" frozen friendships, resumption is not a simple arrangement that may occur anytime. Though on the ideal level severed relations can be mended anytime the parties can be brought together by a third person, in practice this only occurs on important occasions, such as birth, marriage, sickness, death, or another major crisis, when their sense of sharing in the event draws them together without loss of face. Of all these occasions, death alone needs no intermediary for reconciliation.[4]

All these solutions worked out in the women's world are alternative behavior patterns to which women resort in order to preserve the social relations from which they draw the security of support; in this regard, they cannot depend upon men, who neither understand their world nor can partake of it.

Clearly, the same alternatives that can "thaw" frozen friendships or resume them are used to freeze friendships or sever them. Thus, a person who does not wish to put up with the obligations such friendships entail for her can manipulate the same behavior patterns to communicate her withdrawal of support and the end of friendship.

These networks of friendship and kinship provide considerable emotional succor, especially on tragic occasions. When death occurs, women's supportive networks of relatives and friends are immediately activated and are of crucial significance in the adjustive phase that has to follow human loss. Thus, the cultural solution for death, especially of a breadwinner, brings into play other potential sources of security, namely kinship and friendship, and the impressive assurance of complex ties to the community at large.

As soon as death occurs in a family, somebody in the house, usually a friend, notifies all the *ahl, arham,* and close friends, male and female, who are not already present. They immediately suspend all other activities and rush to offer their sympathy and assistance to the family of the deceased. Since early burial is believed to be "the best salute to the deceased," the tasks of preparing the corpse and arranging for the funeral must be attended to first. Upon arrival at the house of the deceased, men and women have different tasks: the women move to the women's quarters, trying to bring comfort, and the men attend to the immediate arrangements. These include securing the necessary papers for burial; bringing in a specialist to perform the ritual of washing the body; purchasing the various kinds of liquids, herbs, and perfumes for the cleansing and the special cloth shrouds in which the body is wrapped; and finally arranging for the burial.

As soon as the corpse is ready, the sons or brothers of the deceased carry it to the mosque, where the congregation performs a special prayer. The procession (men only) then continues to the burial ground, where his or her closest *ahl* lower the deceased into the grave, cover the ground, and then form a line with the rest of their *ahl* and *arham* to receive condolences from those attending.

The support and solidarity that kinsmen extend to those closest to the deceased (i.e., his or her father, sons, or brothers) are formalized by their participation in the condolence ceremonies held for men, during which the Qur'an is recited by a specialist. Men mourners hold these ceremonies for the three following days, beginning shortly after sunset prayer and ending with evening prayer. Such ceremonies usually take place outside the house, where many chairs are assembled to accommodate the guests. A special row is formed close to the entrance of the place and set apart for the condolence line. This line includes all the *ahl* and *arham* who recieve condolence. By joining the line, kinsmen formalize their sharing in the tragedy and reassert their belonging with the closest *ahl* of the deceased.

Among women condolence ceremonies are more elaborate and extend from a period of forty days to four months or even a whole year. Consequently, kinswomen and friends have more occasion to show support to women relatives of the deceased. Condolence ceremonies are preceded by what are called assistance visits, which must be observed by *ahl, arham,* and close friends. Upon hearing the news of death, women, dressed in sober colors of beige, brown, dark blue, and black, rush to the house of the deceased to show their support by comforting the bereaved, helping the widow enter the *'uddah* (a condition of observing tabus which a Muslim woman commences at the death of her husband for a period of four months and ten days), and running the house and making arrangements for serving and attending to the visiting guests.

Because hysterical expressions of grief are considered blasphemous, the first task of kinsmen and close friends of parents, siblings, and daughters of the deceased is to stop women from questioning the will of Allah and to help them temper their grief by a continued faith in Allah and endurance of His will. This they often do by punctuating their comforting words with quotations from the Qur'an. Although men are expected to grieve, they are also expected to, and in fact do, control their grief and rarely have the hysterical outbursts not uncommon among women. Women interpret controlled grief as a sign of Allah's contentment with a woman, "for He has given her the power to endure her pain in patience." To help their bereaved friends reach this state, women also remind them that excessive tears torture the deceased in his grave and must be restrained.

Women friends, *ahl*, and *arham* communicate their sense of sharing in the tragedy by observance of sober colors in their dress and retaining the head cover. They demonstrate their support to the women closest to the deceased (i.e., mother, sisters, daughters) by presentation of mourning clothes as gifts or by money offerings.

Condolence visits begin with the date set for the type of condolence visits the bereaved women choose to hold. Condolence is only received from morning until noon on "condolence days," (Sundays, Tuesdays, and Thursdays), and until the last ten to fifteen years the pattern was to continue receiving condolences on every condolence day until the fortieth day, and sometimes the fourth month, after death. Within the last decade the pattern of receiving condolences on either the third day following death or the first condolence day following death has become more common.

On the set day, all the *ahl* and *arham* of the deceased and sometimes their friends receive condolences. Women struck by the tragedy form a condolence line, which always commences at the right of the entrance to the room, and in the traditional pattern it was always headed by the eldest woman, who could be from the *ahl* or *arham* of the deceased, and who was followed by those closest to the deceased. If the deceased was male, the condolence line must include, from *ahl*, the deceased's mother, mother's sister, daughters, father's mother, father's sister, sister's daughters, son's daughters, and daughter's daughters. From the *arham* it must include wife's mother, son's wife, and brother's wife. Although optional, *ahl* such as brother's daughters usually join the condolence line. As an act of courtesy the following *arham* sometimes sit in the line: daughter's husband's mother and son's wife's mother. Significantly, all the women who must join the line are either those for whom the deceased is the actual supporter or those who, by virtue of the patrilocal system, were dependent on him (such as a son's wife or a son's daughters) or would have been his dependents in case of death of their spouses and sons (for example, the mother's mother; mother's sister; father's mother; father's sister; brother's wife). Therefore, the women who sit in the condolence line—either actual or potential dependents—express the dependant nature of their status in the society which, though ever present, is suddenly brought to the surface by the death of an actual or potential breadwinner. Consequently, the women's condolence line—unlike that of men—always includes friends whose presence confirms their solidarity with the bereaved and reaffirms promises of assistance in the future.

Furthermore, women who sit in the condolence line are formally stating to the community that they are in mourning and that they receive condolence. This is not the message communicated by friends who join the line, for it is recognized that they are there to show support and do not receive condolences. Any person who has any degree of interaction with those in the condolence line must come to pay a visit. Failure to do so terminates all relations between the two parties, irrespective of the strength of their ties. Not only is this norm more radical than it is for men, but it is also more strictly observed. This is perhaps due to the fact that men must do business together and thus cannot afford to terminate a relationship completely for failure to observe social courtesies.

Moreover, women more than men express their varying degrees of friendship obligations in the frequency of their visits to those receiving condolences. For example, close friends are expected to pay one visit—but that is merely the bare minimum for sustaining an ongoing relationship. In addition, delay in these visits, unless resulting from a good excuse such as having been out of town, leads to serious setbacks in friendship and constitutes grounds for the bereaved to "freeze" the relationship and return the same treatment to the other party. The following case is an illustration:

When Murshid died in early June, Huda, wife of one of his business partners and a friend of the widow, was out of town. She returned to Jiddah in the middle of September but did not pay a condolence visit until the last day of Sha'ban (October 19). Although the widow was not home, the visit was considered valid. Two days later, Huda's mother died. None of the women who were in Murshid's condolence line rushed for an assistance visit; nor did they go to the set condolence day or any of the condolence days of the first two weeks. When common friends expressed their disappointment at such failure of duty, Murshid's widow explained: "Nobody is better than the

other. When my husband died, she took her time before coming. She was in Jiddah for almost a month before she decided
to come. We will go to pay a condolence visit, but in due
time."

Similarly, death crises are occasions to thaw relations, whether
between kin or friends, and to solidify and develop a relationship
from the level of close friends to that of "sisters." The following
cases show how these options are carried out:

Halla and Mona were good friends, but due to a major misunderstanding they severed all relations with each other. Three
years later Halla's mother died. Mona rushed to the death-
stricken family as soon as she heard the news. The misunderstanding was not discussed, but Halla understood that by of-
fering her support in an hour of crisis Mona sought to resume
their friendship. Quietly and gradually, Mona began to help
around the house, thereby slipping back into the status of a
close friend. The frequency of her visits during the condolence period made it possible to resume relations at the level
they were before the misunderstanding.

In another case Najlah had a quarrel with her sister's son,
after which visits betwen the households were suspended.
When his wife became sick and went to a hospital, Najlah did
not go until the woman's condition was pronounced critical.
Since Najlah could no longer visit her in the hospital, she
went to her sister's son's house and stayed with the women.
Later that night, his wife died. Najlah then sought the opportunity to resume relations with her sister's sons by observing
every condolence day until the fortieth day after death.

In the third case support and assistance offered following death
deepened friendship ties between the parties involved:

Samiah and Rajiyah were formal friends. Rajiyah did not reciprocate despite Samiah's repeated efforts to increase the frequency of visits between them. When Rajiyah's husband (who
by then was Samiah's daughter's husband's father's brother)
died, Samiah hastened to Rajiyah's house. There she attended
to guests and helped in supervising the condolence ceremony.

She also supplemented this assistance with frequent visits until her departure for Europe three weeks later. Upon her return from her trip four months later, the two women exchanged more visits until finally Rajiyah received Samiah in her informal living room—thereby indicating her acceptance of Samiah as a close friend. When occasions arose, Samiah and Rajiyah exchanged gifts.

On the condolence day, women who form the condolence line cannot leave their places until the ceremony is over. Thus, their kinswomen and close friends assume their roles in running the household: they help prepare the house for the influx of expected sympathizers, welcome and receive them when they arrive. Those kinswomen who show their support to the bereaved by joining the condolence line continue their support by receiving condolences even after the day set for the occasion. Like the closest kin of the deceased, they have to stay home on all the days when condolence is expected and make provision for guests to stay for lunch. This continues until the fortieth day after death, and it may even extend into the fourth month.

Although today ceremonies for receiving condolence have changed, becoming less frequent, expectations of empathy and support from kinswomen and friends have not changed. Women who have these relations with "closest" relatives of the deceased continue to express their empathy through assistance visits and show their support through gifts, services, and frequent visits during the mourning period. Furthermore, they still observe the mourning period with the bereaved. This period varies from four months to one year, depending on the degree of relation to the deceased. For children, husband, parents, and siblings it extends to one year. During the mourning period women do not carry on gift exchanges nor hold celebrations in their homes or attend them at others' homes. They also abstain from wearing colorful clothes, jewelry, and makeup.

Clearly, then, friends and kin are a real source of assistance; the means to generate ties with nonkin and to strengthen them with kinswomen is through *wafa'* as exchange of social visits. The mechanism by which these ties are cemented and reinforced is through *wafa'* as a pattern of reciprocal exchange of gifts and favors.

Just as *wafa'*, in the sense of exchange of visits, is more significant to women than to men, as a pattern of gift exchange *wafa'* plays a more important role for women than for men. Although men exchange gifts in fulfillment of friendship and kin obligations, they do so on fewer occasions and show less commitment to reciprocity. Men present gifts to *ahl* and *arham* and to close friends on occasions of marriage and naming, women also offer goods and services to their exchange partners when sickness or death occurs, and in connection with travels. Five major forms of *wafa'* gifts can be distinguished: *baqshish*, jewelry presentations, *rami*, gifts on special occasions, and services.

Baqshish refers specifically to money donations made to singers and dancers on festive occasions, especially marriage. Strict reciprocity is observed; participation in the *baqshish* is an act of support to the *ahl* of the bride and the groom and is exclusive to women. In the past (more than fifty years ago) marriage ceremonies were numerous, with many occurrences of singing and dancing, each being an opportunity for *baqshish*. Because of the frequency of *baqshish*, only close *ahl*, *arham*, and special friends of the mother of the groom or of the bride "followed her" whenever she gave *baqshish*. The more formal friends restricted their participation in the *baqshish* to the major ceremony on the wedding night held at the bride's natal house, or the following night of celebration held in the natal house of the groom, depending on their friendship with either family.

Although the actual recipient of the *baqshish* is the singer, the donations mark the discharge of an obligation toward the bride's or the groom's mother by the participating guests, whose relationship to the hostess ranges from that of a sister to that of a most formal friend. The amount of the *baqshish* is related to previous exchanges between the parties and to the level of relationship that exists between them. Thus, where higher amounts of *baqshish* are expected, participants are limited to the close *ahl* of the bride,[5] i.e., her mother's mother, her married sisters, and her mother's married sisters. By making these contributions, they affirm their special relationship of maximum mutual support with the bride's mother. The symbolic quality of these donations as expressing the strongest ties among women is reflected by the custom that only those friends who have become "like a sister" to the bride's mother can contribute to this special donation.

Other *baqshish* donations made in the context of marriage celebrations express varying degrees of closeness. For example, female relatives and close friends who join the groom's mother on her visit to the bride's house usually include a somewhat wider group of *ahl* plus a few of her *arham* and close friends. Still wider is the circle of contributors who attend the night of celebration at the groom's natal house following the wedding night. For the groom's mother, they include only her *ahl*, *arham*, close friends, and those formal friends who, by their participation on this occasion, want to enhance and strengthen their ties to her. Clearly, then, the types of *baqshish* donation that women make reflect and define their level of association with the person to whom they show their support.

Jewelry presentations to the bride are exchange transactions between *arham* only (and specific to marriage). These gifts are usually made by the closest male kinsmen of the groom. Sometimes, the groom's mother, and occasionally a close woman friend of hers, may also present jewelry to the bride. The presentations are a way by which the groom's closest kinsmen show their endorsement of the newly created union. Recently, however, marriage ceremonies have been greatly reduced in number, length, and complexity, which has meant a reduction of the occasions for *baqshish* and opportunities for the perpetuation of *wafa'* among friends and kinswomen. However, maintaining *wafa'* relations continues through gifts of jewelry, clothes, and furniture which kin and friends make to the bride and, by association, to the groom. Such presentations either discharge previous obligations or initiate a new level of exchange with the bride, the groom, and their respective families.

The naming ceremony held for a newborn child provides yet another opportunity by which *wafa'* is initiated, expressed, and maintained. On these occasions, *rami* (gifts of gold and jewelry) are exchanged between *ahl*, *arham*, close friends, and those formal friends with whom "similar hands" (i.e., similar favors) have been exchanged. Generally, the circle of women presenting *rami* coincides with the group that donates *baqshish* on behalf of the bride's mother during the celebration at the groom's natal house. However, owing to the greater value of *rami* gifts, these presents convey a more determined effort to strengthen a relationship and serve to recruit new members into an existing exchange network. For the mother of the child, the occasion is the first chance to enter the network as an independent participant in *wafa'* by choosing from among the visitors those women with whom she intends to perpetuate the exchange relationship. Occasions of death, sickness, and travel then provide her with opportunities to reciprocate *rami* gifts received and to cultivate and strengthen bonds of mutual support.

One way of showing support is by rendering services to a *wafa'* partner in need. While all other exchanges strictly follow considerations of reciprocity and status equality (although women of equal social standing sometimes give more than previously received), offerings in the form of services enable women of different status to become *wafa'* partners. The poorer person may return gifts in kind with demonstrations of empathy and gratitude and with work, so that the exchange remains balanced and, at least symbolically, reciprocal. Naturally, the same expressions of support and similar assistance are freely rendered also among those *wafa'* partners who, as *ahl, arham,* or close friends, keep their gift exchange at an even level. But substitution of services for goods received extends *wafa'* networks across status lines. Taken together, the various forms of *wafa'* exchange constitute a system of communication which, through multiple options for involvement, permits the participants to modify their social relationships to suit their personal ambitions and interests.

In the past, unmarried men and women did not participate in *wafa'* except for those exchanges connected with marriage or naming ceremonies of the *ahl*. Because they were minors, their parents provided gifts for them. (Only unmarried women past the normal marriage age exchanged gifts with a multiplicity of friends, *ahl,* and *arham.*) When marriage confirmed their social maturity, they began to participate in *wafa'* exchanges themselves. Younger-generation unmarried women participate in gift exchanges with their own friends, even without their parents' immediate supervision. But as with the older generation, it is marriage that confirms their social maturity, and with it they begin to participate in *wafa'* exchanges.

The gifts received by the bride and groom at marriage represent favors to their parents and *ahl,* and as such are returned by the latter. However, the spouses, as actual recipients of the gifts, have the option of returning gifts to those people with whom they wish to develop ties of exchange. For example, when a woman receives a wedding gift from a friend of her mother's, it is the mother who must reciprocate. If the girl wishes to reciprocate herself, she gives a gift to her mother's friend when the opportunity arises, but this act absolves the mother of the duty to return the gift only when she elects to reduce the level of gift exchange.

Return of gifts is not restricted to occasions similar to those on which they were given, nor is it restricted to an exchange between actual donor and actual recipient. In fact, because women's relationships with *ahl*, *arham*, and friends are punctuated by occasions for *wafa'*, they return a gift on the earliest available occasion after receiving it. For example, if a woman who has fallen sick receives a gift from a close friend, she may bring her a gift when returning from a trip abroad. When the actual donor has no forthcoming occasions to receive gifts, recipients often present a gift to any one of those considered her closest *ahl*. The following is a case in point:

Huda is a middle-generation married woman who had presented gifts to her friends on a number of occasions. Since she had no children herself, her friends had no occasions (marriage or naming) at which to return her gifts. When Najlah, her sister, had a child, all those friends whom she had obliged went to the naming ceremony held for the child and presented a *rami*. Many of these women had no previous exchange of gifts with Najlah, and it was understood that the *rami* were placed for Huda's sake.

The gift thus returned perpetuates the exchange process between actual donor and actual receiver, but it also implicates a third party who has the option to pursue the gift exchange by returning the gift to the donors or to suspend her involvement at this point. The latter course of action is considered by older- and middle-generation women as "eating people's rights" and therefore inappropriate. The following case illustrates how, in the exchange process, obligations proliferate and come to involve more and more people:

Salmah, who is an unmarried woman 40 years of age, has been living with her mother and married brothers. Since her

father's death, she has shared with her mother the first floor
of a four-storey villa. Each of the three married brothers
occupies a floor in the house. Salmah is a friend of Rajhah,
but no gifts were exchanged between them. When Rajhah's
brother's daughter, Aminah, gave birth, Salmah and her
brother's wife, Lama, came to the naming ceremony and offered a *rami*. Then Lama gave birth, so both Rajhah and
Aminah reciprocated by placing a *rami* for her baby. The third
step in the exchange process was taken by Salmah and her
mother, who returned from a trip with a gift for Rajhah. Then,
Najwah, Salmah's second brother's wife, gave birth. Rajhah
wanted to return the gifts received, but she had no *wafa'* with
Najwah. Illness prevented her from attending the naming ceremony. When her health improved, she paid a visit to Salmah,
and the baby was brought down for her to see. She did not
place the *rami* on the baby because she feared that Najwah
might not show it to Salmah as she knew that relations between them were a little strained. When her visit ended, she
left the *rami* on a table near her seat. The message thus communicated was clear: the *rami* was for the baby, but the favor
for Salmah.

Not all relatives qualify as third-party recipients of reciprocal
gifts. In fact, only a limited set of *ahl* are potential third parties to a
gift exchange, and, as such, they reflect the society's conception of
one's closest *ahl*. These include mother, daughters, sons, sisters,
brothers, son's children, daughter's children, sister's children, and
brother's children. (They do not include *arham*, nor do they include
mother's sister or father's sister.) Among these relatives a daughter
receives first priority, followed by a grandchild. Thus, whereas an
actual donor's son's or daughter's wedding is an occasion for the
original recipient to return a gift, only a brother's (or sister's) wedding or a brother's (or sister's) children's naming ceremony are com-
parable occasions. A sister's daughter's wedding or a brother's
daughter's wedding are not selected as good occasions, except in
the absence of all other possibilities or when the original donor has
brought up her sibling's children.

'*Ayb* operates here, too, to bring about conformity to the exchange of visits, gifts, and services. But younger-generation
women are not curtailed by it as were their mothers and grand-

mothers. In fact, they have begun to neglect the traditional obligations that involvement in their mothers' exchange network have
imposed upon them. More important is conformity to conjugal and
motherly duties, which are also covered by the key concept of *'ayb*.
Excusing lapses in traditional expectations, younger-generation
women redefine *'ayb* to exclude these obligations.

Their neglect of traditional obligations, in my view, follows from
their greater mobility and the increased diversity of their domestic
and social duties. For example, we have seen that the women of the
younger generation spend more time with their husbands—a duty
now expected of a young wife. I have, in fact, observed women of
the younger generation leave formal social visits early; their hostess
usually stopped prevailing on them to stay longer as soon as they
said, "This is the time my husband returns home, and I do not want
him to remain alone." Whether younger-generation women use
such arguments as an excuse to go home early is not as important as
the fact that they seldom pay social calls while their husbands have
free time and are at home; and neither do they keep them waiting at
home while they are out on a visit. Indeed, a younger-generation
woman would be criticized for neglecting her husband were she to
linger outside the house. A younger-generation woman criticized
the behavior of a friend's daughter who was known to spend more
time with women friends and *ahl* than with her husband. "She has
no shame. If I were her mother, I would have put an end to this. She
is young and beautiful, but she'll ruin her [married] life this way.
No one tells her not to have friends, but her husband has priority.
Girls these days must be going mad."

Older-generation married couples used to spend much less time
together. They had not only separate quarters but also separate
entertainment. The men went out at sunset to the houses of
friends, where they socialized for some hours before they returned
home to sleep. Even the little time they spent at home was not all
spent with their wives. The reason was the strict separation of the
sexes and the rigid observation of the veil by women guests, which
kept the wife away from her husband as she had to attend to these
guests.

More time spent with a husband offers a wife a better chance to
know him and possibly manipulate him to serve her interests. Al-

though, as I have shown earlier, younger-generation women's behavior is still controlled by their husbands' decisions, they think
they have relatively greater influence over their husbands and that
they have enhanced their autmy.

As an educated woman, a younger-generation mother becomes a
tutor at home—an added task which absorbs a grat deal of her time
and may be more important to her than social visits. Although
almost all younger-generation mothers have nannies to help with
the children, seldom do they leave the nanny without strict supervision.

Another factor enticing young mothers to stay home is the introduction by the current government of television and video cassettes
in the 1960s and late 1970s, respectively. Surely, television provides
entertainment to all three generations, but its effects are different
with the younger-generation women. Whereas it became available
to older-generation and many middle-generation women after they
had been caught up in a multiplicity of friendship relations, most
younger-generation women began their married life when television was already available. Hence, the spare time with which older-
generation and some middle-generation women were originally
faced—and which encouraged exchanging visits—was somewhat
absorbed for the younger women by watching television.

Thus, the greater involvement of women in *wafa'* exchanges
seems to relate to their seclusion of women. By establishing and
maintaining ties of support and assistance, women widen their
social world and find compensation for their relative isolation from
the rest of society. In the process of gift exchange, patterns of reciprocity proliferate and by implicating third parties, extend the networks of mutual obligation. Since only a limited set of *ahl* qualify as
third-party recipients, support obligation gains depth along important kinship lines.

Younger-generation women accept their implication in the exchange process mostly for *ahl* and for some *arham* but are beginning
to ignore obligations that concern friends of the parental generation
in favor of their own friends. This tendency is best understood in
terms of the changed role of the younger-generation wife, who,
along with a greater mobility, has assumed new tasks which leave
her with less time to cultivate friendships. In addition, the closer

husband-wife relationship now offers her greater security, so that her need for other sources of support is somewhat reduced. In the light of such developments one can understand younger-generation women's decreased concern with an involvement in traditional social networks—in some cases to the point where their neglect becomes a source of embarrassment to their natal family.

Conclusions

This chapter has examined the institution of *wafa'* as a mechanism for reducing the isolation and insecurity of *ahl al-balad* elite women. The precariousness of their status must be seen in the framework of the social seclusion in which they are enmeshed by the ideology and practice of the community. By seeking information and news, by exchanging ideas and opinions about trends in women's fashions, by gossiping about other women, and the like, what these women are in effect accomplishing is the establishment, maintenance, and strengthening of friendship ties.

On the other hand, such ties may be reduced or severed completely by disregarding norms of reciprocity in gift, favor, and service exchange. Women will reduce or sever ties when they feel their security is firm enough without them. Whichever strategy is chosen—that is, either to establish and strengthen bonds or to reduce or end them—both formal or informal occasions are available. The most important formal occasions for social visits, as we have seen, include the birth of a child, naming ceremonies, serious illnesses, and death. Informal social visits are characterized by a lessened need for strict reciprocity. Complete severance of ties, it will be recalled, does not occur as a result of lapses in informal social visitations but only upon the formal one of death in the family. Women of lesser status who wish to establish coalitional ties with others of higher standing in the community are not without resources. Although at a disadvantage, such women may substitute service—such as attending to guests—for what they may lack in gifts.

In general, the younger generation appears to experience greater security vis-à-vis their men. This can be seen as a product of

changes in the relationships between men and women. In this regard, the following four trends are important in charting the
changes that have taken place.

1. Younger-generation women are more interested in expanding
the contact time they have with their husbands. This may, in turn,
be attributed to values they have acquired from abroad or to domestic trends. Among the latter may be counted neolocal residence
patterns which have the effect of increasing the amount of time
married couples have to be alone with each other, as opposed to
being in the company of their parents and other senior relatives as
the older ideology of domestic groups encourages them to do.

2. Younger-generation women are more keen to have their children excel in their studies, as competition increases for entrance
into the best schools and for the best jobs after graduation. As a
consequence, younger-generation women have less interest in social visits, deeming it more important to act as teacher-mothers for
their children after school.

3. The availability of television and video cassette recorders has
coincided with the adolescent and adult years of younger-generation women. Social visits become less important as a means for
acquiring information, news, knowledge of recent developments in
the community, etc., or for time management, as women rely more
on television for these purposes.

4. The above departures from traditional behavior by younger-
generation women have been legitimized by a redefinition of the
key concept of 'ayb. It is noteworthy that in the past the obligations
women had to their husbands, children, and a wider network of
ahl, *arham*, and friends did not conflict with one another. For
younger-generation women, however, priority is increasingly given
first to husband and children, then to *ahl*, *arham*, and friends.
Thus, they do not regard it as shameful to fall short on traditional
obligations in the institution of *wafa'*, especially as fulfilling the
obligations may involve them in their mothers' networks.

The implications of these trends for women are significant. The
younger-generation women are not, of course, transgressing the
limits of the norms that the society finds acceptable. They are working within the range of the acceptable, but at the same time they
seem to be expanding the range of what is permissible. Thus it may

be argued that these women are pursuing strategies which enhance their autonomy within the limits of the possible.

NOTES

1. Referred to mockingly by the younger generation as *bashkat,* which means a crony network that meets regularly. It is similar to the Iranian institution known as the *dawrah.* The term *bashkat* had a more specific meaning in Macca in the late nineteenth century, when Hurgronje reported that it referred to an "excursion party," i.e., male friends who collectively arranged for picnics and visits to saints' tombs (Hurgronje, *Mekka,* pp. 43–44).

2. Altorki, et al., "Ritual Reconciliation and the Obviation of Grievances."

3. People refer to this condition in the relationship as *muqata'ah,* "severing relations," and usually specify that the condition will obtain for an indefinite period; hence, the expression *muqata'ah* on life and death.

4. Women explained this state by quoting a saying: *al-mawt faji'ah wa al-'aza' hajamat;* "Death is a calamity and condolence is in haste."

5. This donation has a special name, *nuqtah,* and is distinguished from the *baqshish* by being a bigger sum of money.

CHAPTER FIVE

MARRIAGE STRATEGIES

IN JIDDAH SOCIETY marriage is a rite with rich historical traditions. Since marriage is the means for the reproduction of the community, it is fitting to discuss it in terms of its cultural, social, and economic dimensions. In the following pages, I will examine these matters in the context of ceremony, the perceptions of the principals, the role of parents and other senior kin in the arrangements, the negotiations, qualities sought for in prospective spouses, economic factors involved in partner choice, and political considerations.

The world of kin is generated in part by descent and in part by affinal ties. Behind the affinal ties is the marriage bond itself; and it is the women who are the principal organizers of marriages. As such, they are the principal creators of the resultant kin subgroup which affects the lives of women as well as men in Jiddah society.

While preparing for a coming marriage, older- and middle-generation women sometimes sing a song which summarizes some of the main considerations on which marriages are based. The song depicts a dialogue between the families of the bride and the groom in which the womenfolk in the bride's family wonder about: "This groom who has come to us; left his country [dwellings] and has come to us; left the daughters of his father's brother's son and come to propose marriage to a woman in our neighborhood."

The "groom" then replies: "O, mistress, I have not come for the excellence of your character; nor for your rosy cheeks. We have followed the fame [prestige] of your ancestors; we have brought our gifts and come." This old song highlights marriage as a transaction between families in which the individuals concerned are means to an end. The aim is to create a bond between the two families, as the marriage of a man to a woman widens the net of kin and produces *arham* who are potential sources of support and cooperation. Hence, the attributes of the bride did not motivate the marriage proposal but rather the attributes of the lineage.

In spite of considerable changes in marriage arrangements over the three generations, marriage remains an agreement between families and rarely follows a choice of the two partners. An informant would consider her husband's brother's son to be the ideal marriage partner for her daughter, a view that reflects the traditional preference for patrilateral parallel cousin marriage. Cases of surrogate and cross-cousin marriage, such as those cited in chapter 3, were not frequent. The marriages in all these families in reality reflect the traditional preference for marrying someone from among one's *ahl* relatives, including the children of one's father's sisters (or mother's brothers). But even that preference has lost its former stringency, as more and more people marry children of their parents friends.

Separation of the sexes and seclusion of females give women their role in organizing marriages. As mothers or sisters, they provide the groom and his father with information about marriageable girls and their womenfolk. By transmitting selective information, they can sway men to a course of action in accordance with their own interests. Even now that visual contact between prospective partners to a marriage is possible, the women's role is instrumental; they make the initial selection before recommending a girl to the groom and then maneuvering a way for him to see her.

In the past women did not inform their daughters of a marriage until shortly before it was to take place. As the following case will show, the prospective bride often heard that her marriage had been arranged from girls of her own age, or from some old women with whom she observed only a slight degree of social distance. Usually she had some inkling of what was happening before preparations began for her wedding. However, it was inappropriate for her to express excitement about the marriage or to discuss it with others.

Haniyah is a Hijazi girl 15 years of age and the eldest of her siblings. Next to their natal home lived a Najdite man in his forties who was married with children. One day, Haniyah's mother took her aside and explained that she was an old girl now and she must behave more "wisely." She must start to enter the kitchen and learn how to cook. About the same time Haniyah noticed that women were making and readying clothes, mattresses, and furniture for she knew not whom. As she probed into these activities, she was told by her mother and her father's sisters, who were living with them, that some of these things were for her, and she should not ask more questions. As might be expected, Haniyah tried to probe further. This time, Zakiyah, her father's sister's daughter, an older female who was living with them, confided to her that their neighbor, the Najdite man, had asked her father for her hand in marriage. Haniyah's mother assumed that Haniyah knew, but they did not talk about it much. Haniyah was very unhappy, as she knew that their neighbor was married and had two children. Nevertheless, she next tried to catch a glimpse of him through the shutters and balconies. Six months or so later, the neighbor came to visit their father. Haniyah withdrew to the roof of the house—she wanted nothing to do with a married man. Sara, her 13-year-old sister, was curious to find out more about the "groom" so she sneaked into a room where she could overhear them. The neighbor had come to ask for Sara to marry his younger cousin. Elated at the idea of marrying, Sara rushed back to tell her sister. Again, it was Zakiyah who confirmed the news. Sara also overhead Zakiyah conversing with her mother about the new groom—"I heard him say that he is younger than our neighbor, but quite old, so I was a little scared, but on the whole, I was excited about getting married." Thrilled at the idea of having so many clothes and things, Sara volunteered the news to anyone who wanted to know. Each time she referred to her marriage in front of her mother or her father's sisters, she was reprimanded but forgiven because of her young age. Sara told me that even on her wedding night she had not quieted down. She followed women up and down their three-storey house until she was exhausted. When her mother's brother came to visit them, he found her asleep in a corner of the room and carried her up to the women's quarters. Since Sara's groom was not a neighbor, she had absolutely no idea what he looked like, nor could she learn anything about him beyond what she overheard from the older women in the house.

In this particular case women did not play a role, as both grooms were originally Najdites who had no female kin in Jiddah.

Often, among older- and middle-generation couples, both parents discussed the range of families from which a bride might be selected, as the following cases make clear.

Raji, an older-generation man, moved with his family from Jiddah to Macca. He had a good friend in Macca called Salim. Raji had three sons; the eldest, Zaki, was nearing marriage age. One day, Raji told his wife: "It's really time Zaki got married. I was thinking of the family of Salim. He is a man of excellent character and the family is well known in the community. How about Sanayah, his father's brother's daughter?" Raji's wife had exchanged visits with the women in the family and knew Sanayah as well as Salim's sister, Fatimah. She then replied to her husband: "I do not agree. I know Sanayah. She is not one bit pretty, and why should my son be stuck with an ugly woman? Actually, Salim's sister, Fatimah, is pretty and would be more suitable." "But," her husband answered, "Fatimah is older than Zaki!" [which is discouraged in the culture]. "Never mind," said his wife. "It does not matter— she'll help him mature." Zaki did marry Fatimah. When I asked his mother why she preferred Fatimah to Sanayah, especially in view of the age difference, she told me: "Really, Sanayah was not pretty at all. Besides, Fatimah is good looking, and I like her so much better. You see, I knew how to choose for my son—he has been married for almost forty years. We all live together [in the same compound], and we get along very well."

In the above case, the mother knew the bride-to-be; but sometimes, this was not the case:

Madihah, an older-generation woman who is more dominant in character than her husband, decided that first she would get her two daughters married. With that out of the way, she then wanted her eldest son to marry, because, as she put it, "Marriage ties a man to the house; he will know that he has a wife and child and must return to them. Marriage will keep him from running loose." She talked to her son, who flatly refused. "I am afraid, mother, that she may not be able to live with you." "But, son," she replied, "I am able to live with anyone, even if they were creatures of the underworld." Still, the son did not agree. She then approached his father, but he took his son's side. Needing support, Madihah went to visit Muhammad, the head of the *'a'ilah* and her husband's father's older brother's son. He agreed to speak to her son. Faced with his uncle's insistence, Muhammad conceded. Madihah was now faced with the task of finding him a wife. She talked with the father and the younger son. The father suggested names of good respectable families, and the son told her about a friend of his who was married to a very nice woman from Macca. "They are good people, so why don't you take one of her sisters for Muhammad?" After deliberations, Madihah went with her married daughter to visit the friend's wife and meet his sisters. Later, she chose one of them for her son.

These cases reflect the range of women's involvement in marriage negotiations; the first case is rare, since the groom had no female relatives in Jiddah and therefore had to handle the negotiations himself. In the second case the family was suggested by the husband and agreed upon by the wife. In the third case the mother solicited names of families, and then acted upon these suggestions. Whether the initiative comes from men or from women, the range of families is agreed upon by both; more usually the husband and wife discuss a number of families from which a bride may be sought. Within this range the women move to make their selection, their seclusion making control of this selection possible.

As the third case shows, for some in the middle generation, women—in this instance, the sisters—appeared before other women who were looking for a wife for their son or brother. In other cases, it often happened that middle-generation women "saw" the prospective groom either from a picture or, like their mothers, peering from behind balconies and shutters, as the following case indicates:

Sana, a middle-generation unmarried woman, was of marriageable age. She had a distant paternal cousin, Karim, who was initially meant to marry her older sister but, owing to some misunderstanding, did not. Karim's job took him often on trips to Europe. When he came back from one such trip, his mother repeated her pleas that he get married—this time, to his cousin, Sana. He had not seen her and demanded that his mother and sister arrange for him to meet her. Sana and her mother were then invited to lunch at Karim's mother's home. His sister had arranged for him to be seated in a room where he could get a good look at her. Sana was, of course, not told about this until years after the marriage. Hearing from her son that he liked the girl, Karim's mother went to speak to Sana's mother. She took a picture of Karim which was shown to Sana without her mother's knowledge. Sana had a vague memory of him from the women's quarter when sometimes he came to visit her father. The next time she had a good look at him was from behind the shutters on the balcony, when he came formally to ask her father for her hand in marriage.

It was more difficult for men, especially of the older generation, to peek through shutters and catch glimpses of prospective brides. If a degree of kinship brought her on visits to his home, then he might catch a glimpse of her as she entered or left the house in her veil. Often, they had to rely on the descriptions of their women-folk. Since girls of the older generation usually appeared only in the presence of close friends, *ahl*, and *arham*, women who searched for a bride and who did not belong to this group contrived reasons to pay an unannounced visit and see the girls in the house, if even for a brief while. Then, they would communicate their own opinions to the groom as a description of the girl. Only their appraisal gave an older-generation man any inkling about the appearance of his wife until he saw her on the wedding night.

However, inasmuch as criteria for selecting marriage partners relate more to the status of a family than to personal attributes of the spouses, especially with the older and middle generations, refusing a marriage proposal endangers the relationship between the families and may even terminate it. Consequently, people handle marriage negotiations cautiously in a series of related stages, each minimizing the risk of a final outright rejection.

The process begins with a visit of the groom's womenfolk to "feel the pulse" of the bride's mother. If the latter does not exchange frequent visits with them, they approach the woman on the bride's side they know best and often have her accompany them on their visit. They may or may not disclose the purpose of their visit to this third party, and they usually allude to it in talking with the girl's mother. During the visit, they learn whether or not the girl has been promised to another suitor, or, in the case of the younger-generation girl, whether she prefers to continue her studies before getting married. If the response encourages the next step, a male go-between is selected to approach the men with the proposal. The go-between, who is usually a common friend—and who may, but need not, belong to the *ahl* or *arham* of either party—communicates the proposal to the girl's father, his elder brother, or his father. If the go-between knows none of these men, he asks the nearest *ahl* or *arham* with whom he has strong ties to arrange a meeting between himself and the girl's father or to communicate the proposal to him. At this point, the father of the bride or her father's father can resort to socially acceptable ways to reject the proposal without injuring relations with the other party. In fact, a man is not expected to accept a proposal immediately, as a hasty agreement would show an improper anxiety to get rid of his daughter, a matter which may adversely affect her value in the matrimonial market. Upon receiving the request, the father has the following options to reject the proposal:

1. If he does not care to maintain the relationship he may have with the suitor and with his family, he can damage their relationship by declining the offer immediately and cite as his reasons flaws in the suitor's character, skills, or family affiliations.

2. If he wants to reject the offer but to maintain his friendship with the suitor's family, he can choose one of two standard declarations:

a. He can express his appreciation of the suitor and his family, and then add either that the girl is still too young or that she has been promised to someone else. (This response is credible only if the bride's womenfolk have not already conveyed contrary information.) Moreover, this reply need not be immediate, for, after a period of deliberation, the bride's father can still say that when he discussed the matter with his brother, or his wife's brother, one of them expressed a desire to have the girl for his son.

b. If the groom's womenfolk have received encouraging information, the bride's father can express appreciation of the offer and request time to consult with his male *ahl* or to perform the *khirah* (divination); or, he may suggest that both parties take more time to find out about the other family. As a result of recent changes which have allowed a bride's opinion to influence the proposal, her father may also insist that he needs to sound out the girl's opinion before making a decision.

The bride's father leaves the negotiations at this stage, even if he accepts the proposal. After some time, usually no more than two weeks, the go-between contacts him again to obtain an answer. It is acceptable for the father to stall for still more time, but after the second discussion an evasive answer from him is interpreted as a polite refusal. If the men on the groom's side press him to give a reply, he can resort to any of the following answers, all of which are socially acceptable ways of rejecting marriage proposals without offending the other side.

1. There is no *qismah*, i.e., Allah has not foreordained the union.

2. The *khirah* results are not encouraging.

3. The girl does not wish to be married (a more recent consideration).

Upon receiving a marriage proposal for their daughter, her family members have to assess the groom's character and his family and determine his value on the matrimonial market. This involves investigating a complex of characteristics. Several attributes are summed up under what they call *istiqamah*, a term connoting the observance of religious injunctions to pray, at least the Friday prayer in the mosque, and not to drink or gamble. It also includes observation of social norms relating to the behavior of men and women in the household. Implied in this complex are also moral virtues, such as being forthright and honest in one's dealings with others. The priorities among these attributes for the younger generation have changed, so that today it is recognized that many young men drink and may find it necessary to serve alcohol in their homes. But "excessive" drinking is condemned. Similarly, regular prayer, though still important, has lost its former stringency for the younger generation. Likewise, observation of social norms means accommodating to the new realities in the society and the changes that have taken place.

Education is a quality that has become increasingly important with the middle and especially younger generations within the last twenty years or so. It has become essential that a prospective groom have a college education, as this is recognized as a means of social mobility and financial security. However, while education remains important, within the last decade wealth, or potential wealth, has become a necessary consideration as parents and young girls want to maintain the degree of affluence to which they have become accustomed.

Descent and the reputation of the groom's family are other qualities that the family of the bride considers in a prospective groom. "Good descent" means to belong to known old recognized families and preferably not to be lower descent status than the family of the bride. "Good reputation" refers to the community's assessment of the family on the basis of the behavior of its women and men in conformity to social norms. That, for men, extends to their conduct in the world of business. All these attributes are important to varying degrees in determining the groom's value in the matrimonial market.

Men and women in the bride's family share the task of assessing the groom's character and that of his family. The men inquire about the prospective groom's character from those who know him well, such as remote *ahl*, friends, colleagues at work, and especially *arham*, "because they have lived with the family and know them." Similarly, the women try to inform themselves about the character of his mother and the behavior of his family's womenfolk. When asked for an opinion on this matter, people often curb their generous evaluation of the character of the groom in question because they know that if their views differ radically from the truth, they will later be blamed by the inquiring party. Their responsiblity is proportional to the encouragement they give to the groom or bride's family. If they suggest the name of a spouse to either the parents of the bride or those of the groom and strongly recommend the person, they are more responsible than when the parents themselves suggest a person and ask for their opinion of him or her. Should the realities of married life belie their predictions, the relationships of these men and women to the family who sought the advice become strained.

In the past the bride's opinion did not affect the decision her male agnates made about the marriage proposal. Older-generation women were not consulted before their family agreed to the proposal. The official who drew up the marriage contract often went up to the women's quarter to hear the bride's consent to the marriage, especially if she was a divorcée or if her father was dead. The appropriate behavior for a girl was to remain quiet—which was a sign of consent—or for the womenfolk around her to voice her affirmative response to the man behind the door.

Middle-generation women become more directly involved in the decision. Usually, the girl's mother or relative with whom she observed less social distance talked to her about the proposal received. But her disagreement only delayed a marriage which either or both parents were determined to arrange, as they usually succeeded in persuading the girl. The pressure exerted upon her ranged from a threat of her mother's *ghadab* to her mother's ultimatum to return to her natal family. With the younger generation, close female relatives of the groom have begun to contrive clandestine occasions for the groom to see his bride before the wedding or even before the proposal. They have to maneuver with great discretion in order to avoid offending the bride's family, which might not have agreed to their tampering with tradition in this respect. In such a case, neither the bride nor her womenfolk were aware that she was being seen by the groom, and the matter was openly discussed only after some years of marriage. Similarly, a common friend or women of her age group sometimes smuggled pictures of the groom to the bride. But only recently has visual contact between prospective marriage partners become acceptable, and nowadays, more and more young people insist that they see their spouse-to-be. Despite the recentness of the custom, it has become rare today for younger-generation couples not to see one another before marriage.

Sometimes, when the parents of the girl are known not to consent to her meeting the prospective groom, trickery enables an insistent young man to see the intended, as the following case shows:

Safi, a distant patrilineal cousin of Hamzah, recommended to him and his mother a young girl whom she knew rather formally. Hamzah insisted on seeing her before giving his consent. Since Safi knew that the girl's father would never agree,

she knew that they could only do this discreetly. She therefore
rang the girl to announce that she would visit her the following afternoon, and she arranged for Hamzah to be disguised
as her driver. When the visit was over, and her "driver" came
to fetch her, Safi had thought of a way to get the girl out into
the garden so that Hamzah could take a good look at her. "I
have nice material which I bought downtown, today. It's in the
car; come down, I'll show it to you," she told the girl, walking
her toward the auto. By the threshold of the house, when the
girl was in Hamzah's full view, Safi engaged her in a conversation long enough for Hamzah to see her well. Hamzah liked
the girl. His family made the marriage proposal, and the couple was married.

Over the last decade or so, it has become increasingly acceptable
for both parties to see one another before consenting to the marriage. When intention of marriage is expressed to either parent of
the bride, it is now customary to invite the young man and his
family to visit the girl's family with the set purpose of allowing the
couple to meet and talk to each other. Even when the intention to
marry is not formally communicated, it has today become possible
among these families to permit a brief meeting between potential
marriage partners before a specific proposal is made, as the following case indicates:

Salmah, a middle-generation woman, was actively looking for
a wife for her only son, Samir, who was continuing his studies
overseas. Since he could come home only on brief visits, she
wanted to have a girl ready for him to see. Her wide network
of friends and her son's especially attractive qualities brought
many recommendations from friends and relatives. Amal, a
good friend of hers, told her of a family whom she knew well
and who had three wonderful daughters. So she arranged
with Amal to visit the family. When Salmah saw the girls, she
found them all attractive and was unable to recommend one of
them to her son. Thus, she decided that he should see them
all. Amal knew the girls well and had informed their mother
that Salmah was looking for a bride for her son and that he
wanted to see the girls. A meeting was therefore arranged at
Amal's house, where the three girls, Salmah, and her daugh-

ter went for a visit. When it was time to go home, Samir came
to fetch his mother and sister. He was allowed into the guest
room, had a brief chat with the other guests, and then left
with his mother and sister.

While visual contact has become acceptable at home, prolonged
encounters between prospective partners occur mostly abroad,
where the respective families may be vacationing and the younger
generation are brought together because of kin or friendship relations between their families.

These recent changes have not been fully accepted by the older
generation. One such informant summarized the reaction in the
following words:

> Young people have gone crazy. The groom, they say, wants to
> see the girl. I did not allow my granddaughter's husband to
> see her until the wedding night. We got married that way, and
> so did our daughters, and we are happy. Happiness is from
> Allah; it is not a result of whether they know or see each other.

Adamant as such an opinion is in its adherence to traditions, it
represents an extreme view which is vanishing.

The older generation maintained that in the past (that is, in the
1950s and even the 1960s) there was no visual contact between teen-
aged Saudi boys and girls even when vacationing abroad. "When
such contact occurred, it was accidental and did not lead to further
association between them," they assert. The maintenance of this
fiction was necessary to keep marriage an arrangement between
families and to reduce individual initiative on the part of prospective spouses. Because kinship plays an important role in structuring
social and economic relations in Jiddah society, marriages could not
be allowed to slip into the hands of prospective spouses. The fiction
is then best explained as an attempt to reconcile the realities of
change with a guiding principle of the social structure.

The parental generation of today's teenagers does not perpetuate
such fiction. While they, too, seek control over the marriages of
their sons and daughters, the claim that no visual contact takes
place between the sexes is no longer credible. Instead, they ac-

knowledge the reduced separation of the sexes and seek to control its consequences.

Whereas in the past neither parent took the initiative in marrying off his or her daughter, today both men and women are taking a more active role in this domain. In the past the norm was that single girls of marriageable age should not appear in big social gatherings, for this could be interpreted to mean that her parents were soliciting a husband for her, which in turn implied an inability to support and guard her. This is a matter which adversely affects the family reputation and may reduce their daughter's value in the matrimonial market. Today, middle-generation women, with the full agreement of their husbands, accompany their marriageable daughters to weddings and big receptions in an attempt to bring them to the notice of the community at large and especially other women who have eligible sons or relatives.

Another important change is the woman's role in her own marriage. Younger-generation women are more actively involved in discussions of the proposals than their mothers were; and their decision largely determines its acceptance or rejection. Even on the ideal level the opinion of a prospective bride must be obtained before drawing up the marriage document, and the woman's refusal may suspend the whole process. Actually, the girl's father, or, in the event of his death, another *wakil* (guardian) often communicates her consent to the religious official who draws up the contract, but he rarely does this against her will. Similarly, cases which occurred in Jiddah during fieldwork indicate that some women, outside these families, who are past the normal marriage age or nearing it accept a proposal despite their father's objections. These are always cases where the suitor is likely to offer the last chance for a girl to get married, and where her father has declined his offer and those of suitors before him because he needs the daughter's labor in the house, or her income if she is employed or wants to gain the marriage payment from an aged suitor.

In some of these cases the women are advised to resort to the *qadi* (a judge who administers *shari'ah* law), who can disregard the father's objections to the marriage. Such encouragement is always conditional on the "good character" of the suitor and his observance of Islamic practices. If the woman is a widow or a divorcée, her consent is even more important—a right given to women under the *shari'ah*.

So far, marriages in defiance of parents are rare indeed among the elite families, though the growing awareness of the possibility of such a course allows young people to pressure reluctant parents to give their consent. Only two of the younger-generation women in the sample have yet chosen this alternative, perhaps because parents and daughter alike see a woman's participation in marriage arrangements to be restricted to giving or withholding consent, not to selecting a partner. Indeed, for a woman to initiate the marriage proceedings presupposes knowledge of the suitor and the possiblity of love between the partners—a matter still unacceptable to the family and a threat to arranged marriages.

That most of the younger-generation women who have been educated abroad do not contribute to a more radical departure from tradition must be understood in terms of the advantages they perceive in their society. Women of the younger generation see advantages in the relative freedom of choice that liberated Western women enjoy in the countries they visit. Nevertheless, this realization has not geared them toward open defiance of traditions, except in rare and isolated cases. Whereas all of them remember the difficulties experienced when they first returned to Jiddah, by the period of fieldwork many had adapted to the norms of their society. The "boredom" they often complained about results largely from their seclusion from public life. As such, it is greater than the boredom experienced by a girl of their own age group who has spent most of her life in Jiddah and who has not experienced "the world outside the house." This feeling appears to be the extent of their dissatisfaction. Whereas they complain about parental control and restrictions on their mobility, many see advantages in the financial and emotional security which their networks of kin and friends grant them. A younger-generation woman who had been educated in British schools in Egypt but had not gone to college talked about her fifteen-year marriage:

> I did not see my husband, Hazim, when he proposed. I had once caught a glimpse of him when he came to visit my uncle's house. The women in his family hardly visit us, since they live

in a different city. The marriage proposal was due to the efforts of my father's cousin, who is also Hazim's older brother's friend. Because Hazim was studying in the United States and also because his family prefers to spend their summer in Ta'if [a summer resort in Saudi Arabia], we never had a chance to see each other abroad. When my father asked me about marrying Hazim, I said: "I don't know the man but I trust you. If you inquire and find out that he will be a good husband for me, I shall accept your advice."

Explaining her attitude, she added:

You see, I knew my parents love me and want the best for me. It is not possible that they would give me to a person who is not good. I accept their judgment because they have better means of assessing his character [i.e., obtain information from men who know him well]. And, after all, if I am unlucky and mine turns out to be a case of a badly matched couple, I can always return to my father's house and live the life of a queen!

This respectfully submissive attitude toward parents is not shared by most of the present teenagers. They insist on seeing and knowing the groom-to-be, and they are more involved in the decisions that affect their marriage. Young girls discuss openly with their mothers and fathers the qualities of the intended groom. However, in expressing their preferences, these women seldom allude to "love" as a precondition for marriage. Rather, they stress the importance of knowing a man's character (if only through a few meetings between them in the presence of others) for reaching a decision about the marriage proposal.

"Love" implies freedom of choice by the marriage partners and is a threat to parental control. "Love" also implies a clandestine relationship before marriage, and that certainly has an adverse effect on a woman's honor and on that of her kinsmen. Thus, it remains unacceptable as a reason for marriage arrangements.

All parents of all generations in these families express a preference for an early marriage for girls (17–20 years). They cite the challenge which education, travel, and contact with other societies, among other factors, have brought to traditional norms governing women's behavior. In the words of one middle-aged man who has three daughters: "It's really better to get a girl married early. My daughter, Halla, got married two years ago. She was then seventeen. With the kind of calamities young people get into, it's best to marry early."

Once the families reach an agreement on the marriage proposal, they set a date for the ceremony during which the marriage document is drawn up, and the *mahr* is presented. I have chosen the Arabic term in preference to "bride price" because the latter does not properly describe the meaning of the transaction. Unlike the African practice, where property and valuables are given to the bride's father or lineage head, the Islamic practice is defined "as payment which the wife is entitled to receive from the husband in consideration of the marriage."[1] Although the bride's father or his surrogate may actually accept the money and property, they use these to purchase the bride's trousseau, the total cost of which often exceeds the *mahr* received.

The *mahr* was, and in these families still is, often paid by the groom's father. For older- and some middle-generation marriages, the standard for a girl was 100 gold pounds—then equivalent to 4,000 Saudi riyals, or approximately $1,500.00. With this money, about forty or fifty years ago an older- or middle-generation bride furnished two rooms in her husband's father's residence and provided complete kitchen equipment in addition to her personal clothing. With the middle-generation women these provisions increased to include the furniture for two bedrooms, a dining room, a living room, the salon, and the kitchen.

In the 1970s, the value of the *mahr* for younger generation marriages increased to an average of S.R. 10,000–15,000. Informants explained that the increase was due to the rising cost of the clothes and furniture which the bride provides. In most marriages, the groom's father still pays the *mahr*, but there are a few cases where the groom himself has made the payment. This tendency has led to a general complaint among young men not of those families that marriage expenses have soared beyond their means.

At that time these were exorbitant demands upon the resources of young Saudi men, and they induced many—though not from among these families—to marry girls from Egypt and Lebanon, for whom expenditures were greatly reduced. This loss of marriageable young men to women from other countries has caused alarm among parents with mature daughters in the elite families. Consequently, an innovation has gained acceptance whereby the bride's father asks the groom to make a minimal payment but to furnish his own house. The initiative must come from the bride's father, since it is considered bad taste and *'ayb* to negotiate the *mahr*. (In fact, the increased sums were not demanded by the bride's fathers but represented voluntary payments in excess of traditional rates by a few grooms who thereby raised the general standard.)

Cases of settlement with the groom are still uncommon. When they occurred, they always involved an educated young man who married into a wealthier family. His education, positively valued as a means of social mobility and an important determinant of his value in the matrimonial market, made him desirable to the girl's family, who in turn made concessions to facilitate the marriage. A match that is desirable in these terms also means that the bride's father may seek out the groom. However, since the initiative should come from the groom's side, the bride's father who "sets his eyes" on a good groom must attract him subtly, or even indirectly through friends who recommend the girl. This is done so as not to compromise his daughter's value by giving the impression that he wants to get rid of her. A man does not take such a step without consulting his wife. In fact, the prospective groom may be suggested to him by his wife. The daughter is brought into the deliberations only after the young man's positive intentions are determined.

While the *mahr* is still the property of the bride, she often leaves it to her parents to administer. But whereas older-generation women could not inquire or discuss their *mahr* with others, younger-generation women know the sum paid and sometimes even control its use. Today, the *mahr* among these families has reached exorbitant figures that start from S.R. 100,000 (equivalent to $33,000.00) and can reach S.R. 200,000. This sum is usually paid by the groom's father and is now placed in a bank account for the bride and not used for her trousseau. Providing the house and furniture for new couples may be done by either parents of the groom or of the bride and appears to be related to their relative wealth and willingness to indulge their sons and daughters. Furnishing a house today means

European furniture of the highest quality, Persian rugs, silver, the finest china, videos, and an expensive car—sometimes a Rolls Royce. This staggering expense is a reflection of the great wealth that the recent boom has brought to these families.

These considerations about *mahr* lead directly to the consideration of marriage in its economic context. Here, it is important to reiterate that marriage in Jiddah society is perceived essentially as a bond between two families, and not simply as a tie between two individuals. To be sure, a number of changes have been documented for the younger generation in particular which appear to show the adaptation of marriage patterns to the growing social individuality of women. But this should not lead one to lose sight of the fact that despite these shifts, marriage remains a social, not an individual, contract.

The bonds between *arham* created by marriage are important for both women and men. As has already been shown for women, *arham* are secondary only to *ahl* relations, and both provide women with a network of support, assistance, and emotional succor. *Arham* assume leading roles in life cycle events and become partners to an exchange process that extends from visiting to providing financial assistance when needed. One can argue, however, that these consequences still fall within the domestic world.

Affinal ties affect the men's world in equally significant ways. To begin with, it is not unusual for economic cooperation to follow or sometimes to precede marriage ties between families, each set of ties thus reinforcing the other. The history of cases of such marriages among these families points to the strength and continuity of affinal ties even if marriage takes place in only one generation, as the following case indicates:

> The Samiri family was engaged in commerce. Nasr, the head of the lineage, was born in Jiddah from Indian descent toward the end of the nineteenth century. He had become successful in the trade of sugar, rice, and grain. The Bahi family has two sons who were born in Jiddah about the first decade of the twentieth century. They, too, had formed their own enterprise, importing grain, rice, sugar, tea, etc. The elder son from the Bahi family married Maha, the sister of Nasr. A year or so later, a company for imports was established between the two

families. Shortly thereafter, Maha died, leaving no children. Her widower later married another woman and produced a line of sons who up to this day continue the company operations together with the son of Nasr. The Bahi family, however, also has many enterprises which it holds independently and has established and developed over the last twenty to thirty years. The Samiri family has been less fortunate. The founder, Nasr, had two sons, but the elder died during Nasr's life and was survived by three daughters of the middle generation and one son of the younger generation. Since the family business was in Nasr's name, his son left very little inheritance for his offspring, who, upon Nasr's death had no legal rights to the company's shares. The only beneficiary from the Samiri family was Nasr's second son, who still continues to be a partner with the Bahi family in some of their enterprises. No further marriages have taken place between the two families.

According to informants, relations between older-generation men of the two families were "just like two brothers." There were, of course, frequent visits and support in crisis situations. For example, when Nsar's son fell sick and had to travel to Cairo for treatment, his one-time sister's husband from the Bahi family accompanied him for the duration of the treatment. Today, among the younger generation of both families, amicable relations exist, but there is neither the frequency of visits nor the expectation of support.

It cannot be conclusively suggested that the joint business transactions involving some of these families are all accompanied by marriage ties among them. The best evidence shows that 2 of the 13 families had joint ventures with affines; 3 with nonaffines; and at least 4 with both affines and nonaffines.[2] Interestingly, all these enterprises have to do with commerce and not with the pilgrimage business.[3] It must also be pointed out that all these enterprises date back to the older generation. However, this is not to suggest that joint business ventures are no longer concluded with *arham* in present-day Jiddah society. Whereas it is hard to get exact figures, it is not uncommon for business and *arham* links to occur together. For example, in a recent case, an older-generation man, Rashid, had a piece of land which, due to the expansion of the city, had become of excellent commercial value. He planned to build a high-rise that would serve as offices and a commercial center. Lacking the necessary cash, he sought Hani, who is an affine (i.e., Rashid's wife is Hani's mother's sister). Hani provided the capital for the project, and in return he now receives rental income from the building for five years, after which all reverts back to Rashid.

In addition to formal business, many cooperative financial enterprises are undertaken by these families. Those who now engage in commerce in the past relied on trade of maize, barley, dates, and sometimes rice from Basra, Iraq; tea, sugar, cardamom seeds, rice, and spices from Bombay and Calcutta in India. In each of these towns they had their agent who would sometimes advance merchandise and accept pay in installments. Initially, merchants sent their dues in gold with a "trusted messenger" who, especially at the time of Ashraf rule, smuggled the gold out. There were, of course, cases of theft, and sometimes confiscation of merchandise of Nejdite merchants by Ashraf rulers. The Banque d'Indochine, one of the oldest in the city, became an alternative to "personal messengers" as the city became more tied to world markets.

To raise the necessary funds for importing merchandise, some of the merchants would first resort to *ahl* and *arham* kinsmen, as well as to wealthy friends. In return for loans, the suppliers would become partners in the profit. If such kin and friends could not provide the needed funds, then merchants resorted to other merchants known to them. It is difficult to get accurate figures on the size of these transactions, but male informants reported on, for example, a large shipment of 30,000 tons of rice which would cost 30,000–40,000 gold pounds. While there were few merchants who could individually put up these sums, a more secure and common pattern was to chip in with others.

Also common is the assistance of *ahl* and *arham* in modern business ventures. For example, one of these families has the general agency for several makes of American cars. As *arham* links tied them to another family, they subcontracted some lines of cars to their *arham*.

The political implications of this relative financial power are not clear and cannot be well documented. Part of this relates to the nature of the political regime, where members of the house of Ibn Sa'ud keep the largest share of political power for themselves and their *arham*. It is true, however, that some of the men in these families were either in the center of power (by holding important governmental posts) or had direct access to those in positions of power and thus had power by association. Kinship ties and obligations reach into the political arena as those in power or close to it offer employment and facilities to their kinsmen, both *ahl* and *arham*.

It must be pointed out, however, that over the three generations of this study there is a *relative* decline in the importance individuals attach to kinship ties. Whereas *ahl* links, particularly in the *'a'ilah*, still remain strong, there is a tendency for *arham* links to be narrowed down to the immediate lineages involved and not to proliferate to include separate *arham* of each lineage, as they did in the past. But the *arham* bond is still significant not only for the generation involved (as, for example, sister's husband and wife's brother) but especially for the offspring.

On the whole, honoring kinship obligation is a cultural ideal. it is also a religious duty which men and women in the families try to observe. Toshihiko Izutsu, whose classic study attempts a contextual and semantic explanation of moral concepts of the Qur'an, elucidates the concepts of "good works," righteousness, and their antitheses. Delineating what constitutes good works in Islamic thought, Izutsu states that the Qur'an "enumerates the following five elements: to worship none save God; to be good [i.e., kind and benevolent, *ihsan*] to parents, near kinsmen, orphans, and the needy; to speak kindly to everyone; to perform the prayers; and to pay the alms."[4]

Kinsmen include both *ahl* and *arham*, and Saudis differentiate between the two by using a different term for each. There is no doubt that in the cultural model of the *ahl al-balad* elite, *ahl* are conceived of as "closer" than *arham*. Although there is an expressed patrilineal bias, yet, as explained earlier, *ahl* relatives are reckoned bilaterally and constitute an important part of ego's world of kin.

The *arham* of the father are, of course, the maternal kin of his offspring. They constitute what the people call *khawal* (from the term *khal*, meaning mother's brother). In a society that allows polygyny, defining the maternal links becomes important to differentiate half-siblings—but in the families studied it was considered important for establishing the compatibility of the families that have entered into the marriage. Whereas by virtue of patrilineal descent an individual takes membership in his father's lineage, mother's descent, if considered lower, can sometimes adversely affect prestige, as the following case indicates:

> Samiah is the daughter of an important businessman who was highly regarded by the community. Her mother had been a concubine who was set free upon conceiving her. The father had also married other women and produced a number of sons and daughters. All Samiah's half-sisters of marriageable age married into families similar to their own. But Samiah, now nearing thirty, is still unmarried. When I asked women informants why an attractive young woman like Samiah is still not married, they explained: "Samiah's case is difficult, because she wants to marry into the same families as her half-sisters. But Samiah's mother is a slave. Many men [of the same standing] don't accept that in a wife."

If, on the other hand, a marriage is with a compatible family, the offspring gain from the status of their maternal kin. As a middle-generation man put it, "Of course I must consider the family into which my son marries. First of all, they'll be our *arham*. Also, the *khawal* of my son's children must be respected people in the community—people whom the children can be proud of."

Over and above their bearing on ego's status, the cultural model of *ahl* kin includes relatives reckoned bilaterally and hence *arham* bonds become especially significant when they are "transformed," so to speak, into *ahl* ties. We have already seen that kinship predominates as a structural principle in the society and have seen its expression in solidarity and support among kinsmen. This support permeates the social world of women and men and may be elaborated into economic transactions between men and perhaps some political influence where the system allows for it.

Conclusions

Here, as elsewhere in the Middle East, regularities in marriage choices cannot be understood simply in reference to the rule.

Hildred Geertz, for example, has shown that for Sefrou (Morocco), marriage decisions must be understood as also the result of pragmatic considerations of men and women in the families of the prospective spouses. Such considerations include social and economic advantage as well as industriousness and domestic harmony.[5]

I have argued that marriages in Jiddah society represent family bonding among groups seeking to augment their symbolic and material capital. Marriages frequently permit members of the community to establish and expand commercial ventures. This is manifested both in joint ventures between families and *arham* and in lending money. Marital alignments also can have political consequences, as political influentials have the option of extending jobs and access to relatives by marriage.

While men try to convert marriages into political and economic alliances that have an impact in the larger community, the women are more interested in enlarging the domain of their own autonomy vis-à-vis their men. This is best seen in terms of women's roles as the chief "brokers" of marriages. Without their participation, men would not have enough information at their disposal to create the alliances they ideally would like to have. It can be seen that, to the extent that marriages are the chief means by which a community reproduces itself, women enjoy a major part of the responsibility for arranging that reproduction.[6]

The women in these families are initiators of discussion, disseminators of factual information, conveyors of images and subjective feelings about looks and personalities, facilitators of meetings between parents of prospective spouses, and even engineers of disguised meetings between the principals. Younger-generation women increasingly demand a say in the future marriage plans, including the right to veto parental choices and even to meet a potential groom—if only briefly and in the company of others. The ability of some of these women, also, to control the use of the *mahr* represents a gain in their stature in comparison to older- and middle-generation women.

As we have seen, marriage strategies involve a number of considerations for those involved. On one level, i.e., that of the *'a'ilah*, marriage to kin and nonkin alike aims to maintain and expand the *'a'ilah*'s economic capital and has sometimes resulted in joint eco-

nomic ventures. Such marriages were between equals in some, if
not all, of the criteria which determined the elite status of these
families. This set the boundary of choice for compatibility between
families and was always agreed upon by both men and women in
the initial stage of marriage choices. Conforming to the various
criteria of elite status, these choices also maintain and expand the
'a'ilah's symbolic capital.

On the level of the domestic group, the power relationship which
obtains is also relevant to the marriage choice made. Women seek
to maintain their power in the household by selecting wives for
their sons who will be obedient, will not disrupt the existing authority relationships, will not make extravagant demands on the
household budget, and will be their allies in evading some of the
restrictions placed on women. Domestic tension, if allowed, would
threaten the unity of the domestic group with fission—as the young
women begins to voice her independence in the form of neolocal
living arrangements. With the recent trend to neolocal residence,
these considerations give way to a more general consideration
among women for a girl who will show her proper deference to her
in-laws and thus maintain the integration of the *'a'ilah*.

Generally, the strategies for women do not override those of men,
for men and women usually agree on the circle from which a mate
will be chosen. Because marriage bonds have consequences for the
society at large, they still remain primarily an arrangement between families and involve minimal initiative on the part of the
couple. The ideology of parent-child relationships censors chal-
lenges and defiance of parents' wishes through the concept of
ghadab, which operates more effectively on women than on men.
Especially important has been the adaptation of Islamic teachings to
the "social individuality" of the woman in regard to her marriage.
While her participation in the selection of her husband is severely
curtailed, her family must obtain her consent to the proposed
match. Her power to veto her agnates' decisions, or, under rare
conditions, even marry against their wishes, gives her a degree of
control over her life that her mother never had and may not even
have sought.

Despite these changes, however, women's mobility outside the
house remains limited. Theoretically, and sometimes actually, no

woman, irrespective of age or status, can go abroad without the written permission of her legal guardian, i.e., either the father or the husband. Similarly, women's autonomy has increased but is not equal to that of men. Exceptions are a result of status rather than sex differentials, for example, when a man in these families deals with a women of clearly superior status (e.g., with royalty or even with a woman of greater wealth). In all the cases I have observed men showed deference to such women, obeyed them, and sought them with pleas to facilitate a transaction with the government. These women, through their husbands, can influence events.

Nonetheless, men's higher status is sanctioned by the ideology and is expressed in positions of economic and political power which men occupy exclusively. In the last analysis, their control is backed by law, supported by the political system, and guarded by the coercive power of the state.

NOTES

1. John L. Esposito, *Women in Muslim Family Law.*

2. This evidence comes only from the information on their business activities that is publicly known or that I was able to find out about. There may be many other ventures that I was unable to learn of.

3. The pilgrimage traffic has been controlled for many years by the same families. However, businesses involved in the pilgrimage traffic have declined in profitability, so that new joint ventures do not get involved in it, and the traditional families who have regulated it are increasingly turning to other sources of revenue.

4. Toshihiko Izutsu, *Ethico-Religious Concepts in the Quran,* p. 205.

5. Clifford Geertz, et al., *Meaning and Order in Moroccan Society,* p. 370.

6. The analysis of marriage choices owes its main thrust to Bourdieu, *Outline of a Theory.*

CHAPTER SIX

IDEOLOGY AND STRATEGY

A MAJOR UNDERLYING POINT of this study is that social change articulates with ideological changes in specific ways. Although at times in this book ideology and strategy have been discussed as if they operated autonomously, it is important to emphasize their interrelationship. We speak of an ideology as a system of belief which serves the individual for the mental reconstruction of the real world in which he or she acts. It is a system of beliefs that incorporates a range of meaning, and individuals refer to particular facets or symbols of that meaning system in order to best orient their behavior. A strategy, on the other hand, is a rational calculation of behavior that an individual should follow in order to advance his or her interests.

It will be clear that no strategy can be chosen in a vacuum. Thus, a person who selects a certain line of conduct cannot meaningfully do so without reference to a system of beliefs to channel that action. A strategy is a course of action plotted within the framework of a set of cultural maxims. Its relative morality, immorality, success, or failure is gauged by other social actors who refer to that same set of maxims, though they may differ in their specific understanding of them. The individual, therefore, has a great deal of strategic scope to pursue interests; but although his or her strategy may be idiosyncratic, for it to be truly social, and hence successful, it can never be inconstruable—others must be able to understand it as a variation on cultural themes.

In the case of domestic groups in Jiddah, strategies to enhance interests are adopted within the context of an ideology of these groups. This ideology stresses: (1) male dominance; (2) women's subordination and seclusion; (3) children's obedience to parents; (4) solicitous attention to kinship groups; (5) the veiling of women; (6) the attribution of rationality to men and emotionalism to women;

(7) the marriage of women and men to preselected partners; (8) property inheritance that favors males.

The strategy adopted by women in *ahl al-balad* elite domestic groups differs according to the generational differences, although more similarities may be found between the middle and younger generations than between either of these and the older generation. The common principle underlying the strategies chosen is that, for all their variation, in each case strategy in fact represents an interpretation of the ideology by the individual or group.

It is clear that the traditional model makes it impossible for women to choose certain strategies. Thus, for example, it would be out of the question for them to demand an end to male domination, to establish women's full participation in the society and economy, to institute an egalitarian relationship between children and parents, to place the exclusive focus of social relations upon nuclear families, to discard veiling, to claim equal rationality to men, to take the initiative in selecting marriage partners, to reconstruct inheritance patterns in favor of equality with men. These represent polar opposites of ideological principles and are, for that very reason, beyond realization.

But ambiguities and contradictions exist within key concepts of the belief system. It is thus possible for women to reinterpret the ideology by choosing to give nuance to particular significations (and not others) within the range of meanings the ideology encompasses. Strategy being a matter of choice and perceptions, *ahl al-balad* elite women and men can then play an active role, through choices that they themselves make, to interpret or otherwise modify patterns of meaning featured in the established ideology.

Male domination therefore becomes tempered male control. Women's seclusion is altered to conditional segregation. Children's subordination to parents becomes qualified dependence upon them. Extreme solicitousness for extended kinship groups becomes redirected attention to conjugal relations. Women's veiling becomes partial covering of the body. Men's claim to exclusive rationality outside the home evolves into contingent rationality for women outside the home. Preselection of marriage partners for women becomes consensual participation in the arrangement by women. And male property control is supplemented by female management of the household budget and rights to knowledge about inheritance or even its control.

What makes it possible for these absolutes to become modified into contingencies? A major contention of this book is that ambiguities and contradictions within the sets of concepts of *dhanb/'ayb* and *ghadab/rida* are what have permitted women to make the changes they have initiated. To be sure, the ambiguities and contradictions, per se, are insufficient to enable them to do this. Social and economic trends that have been occurring in the kingdom, including changes in education, cultural diffusion from other parts of the Arab world, foreign travel, and rapid economic growth have all been necessary elements of the ideological changes in question.

To show this process at work, let us focus upon veiling. Veiling was once interpreted in an absolute manner; it was a presumption that women would veil to all men but their husbands, children, and relatives whom they could not marry. But older-generation women began to relax strict veiling practices before older male servants in the home during their husband's absence. This soon gave rise to partial unveiling outside the home, a development facilitated by the announcement on the part of the *'ulama'* that women need not veil their faces or cover their hands when in the holy mosque in Macca. With the passage of time, middle- and younger-generation women then came increasingly to relax veiling practices yet further as Western-style shopping areas were established in the city. A similar development occurred with the increasing use of automobiles. While younger-generation woman have participated more directly than their middle-generation counterparts in the changing veiling practices, the later have been involved to a degree. We thus can see that shorter cloaks came to replace the traditional form of the veil. Middle- and younger-generation men have more and more encouraged their wives to unveil partially while in cars outside the city center.

Middle- and younger-generation women and men have adjusted the veiling criteria another step as the married members of these groups have participated in mixed gatherings. Again, the middle-generation women have been somewhat more reluctant to do so, confining their participation to mixed gatherings abroad. The younger-generation women have unveiled and attended mixed gatherings even in Jiddah, although they have continued to dress conservatively in order to maintain the standards of decency expected of Saudi women.

If we look at these developments as stages, we can see that patterns once viewed as religiously sinful have become not sinful nor even shameful from a social point of view but in fact acceptable. One meaning of what constitutes *dhanb* or *'ayb* has come to override another. Moreover, it must be mentioned that in this evolution, men have played a key role. For, in encouraging modified observance of female segregation, they, in fact, made it easier for women to "come out" into society more; and in turn this made it more possible to promote women's education. At the same time, increased educational opportunities served to modify yet further the traditional segregation practices.

The justification given for educating young girls when the government introduced this reform in the early 1960s was that education would help these girls be better Muslims and enable them to teach their own children to become so. But the men who at that time were predisposed to educate their daughters did not rationalize this step exclusively on that ground. They no doubt accepted the argument that education would enable their daughters to become more worthy Muslims, but they also had in mind the general principle that education befits one's family members, in accordance with the saying attributed to the Prophet: "Seek knowledge, even unto China."

Consequently, they sent their daughters (and sons) not just to local but also to foreign schools. In acquiring new values, boys came to be skeptical of older views on educating both sons and daughters. Later, as men, they acted upon changed values in regard to the education of their own children. Girls came back home with new perspectives on their roles as future wives favoring joint decisions with their husbands on the future of their offspring. To a degree, then, some male and female functions became fused, which, with the preference for neolocal residence patterns, combined to give new influence to women in domestic groups. As this process unfolded, female enrollment in the kingdom rose dramatically, leading to the entry of women into professions such as education, health, and welfare. Additionally, with their new-found awareness, women have become increasingly assertive in regard to their property rights. To be sure, there is a limit to their emerging autonomy. They may become teachers, for example, but only of other women. Yet, as these examples show, the concept of *'ayb,* which in the traditional culture would have deterred women from these moves, has been so reinterpreted that they have been realized.

A similar transition may be traced with regard to different interpretations of *ghadab* and *rida* as far as parent-child relations are concerned. The older elite ideology insists on absolute obedience of child to parent. This has meant accepting parental authority over all substantive areas of children's lives and has implied certain proprieties. For example, children were expected to stand when their parents entered the room; they were not allowed to cross the room with shoes on while their parents were seated on the floor; children were always expected to initiate salutations upon seeing their parents after an interval, to keep their voices low in discussions with them, to kiss their hands as a sign of respect and deference, etc. To do less was viewed as shameful and likely to incur their parents' discontent. A child's defiance on a more basic issue would generate parental *ghadab.*

The children of all three generations have moved away from that model in the following ways: (1) relaxing certain criteria of obedience and deference to mothers (boys more so than girls); (2) seeking the support of mothers to change the disciplinary commands of fathers (girls more so than boys); (3) obtaining the privilege of staying out longer on outings; (4) for married offspring, insisting upon physically separate entrances and exits in the household in order to reduce parental interference, or moving to a totally different area of the city for the same purpose; (5) requesting to be sent abroad for education; (6) demanding the right to see prospective spouses prior to the drawing up of the marriage contract; (7) reducing contacts with the network of the parents' friends and relations.

It is argued here that children of the three generations are, in fact, continuously renegotiating their privileges while trying to avoid their parents' *ghadab.* Testing the limits of parental *ghadab* is possible because this is not a monolithic concept but one based on a continuum ranging from temporary rejection (there being no disinheritance possible under Islamic law) to outraged fury, to anger, and finally to discontent. Thus, the negotiation probably is best seen as occurring over those issues mainly provoking parental discontent. Hence, if boys smoke in front of their mothers or if girls raise their voices in discussion with them, this has been achieved through trail and error, give and take. But *ghadab* is not so flexible as to be endlessly manipulable by children seeking, for example, to select spouses they know would be rejected by their parents.

In the cases of veiling and children's obedience to parents, the principle has been maintained and adhered to by members of all three generations. Yet, how much veiling or obedience and in what context have changed. Relatively wide latitude exists for individuals to follow a different course of action. Old meanings of veiling and obedience have yielded to new ones without the abandonment of the essential principles.

The ideology of these domestic groups is predicated on the seclusion of women and asymmetrical power distribution between males and females, old and young. Both principles are maintained and reinforced by the working of the social concept of *'ayb* and its corollary, the religious concept of *dhanb*. These two concepts grade nicely with one another, whereby some infractions bring social criticism and also divine punishment. They are further enforced by the modesty code, which makes the behavior of the women their own responsibility and also that of men. The double jeopardy in the modesty code touches upon male dominance and, at the same time, the vulnerability of men through the behavior of their women. Beyond its impact on men, in its various extensions the modesty code restricts the mobility of women and narrows their horizons.[1] The findings here are consistent with those in other Islamic and Middle Eastern societies, where the honor of men is vested, partially, in the behavior of their women.

It is clear that the two concepts of *'ayb* and *dhanb* form an indispensable part of the elite ideology in Jiddah society. As was shown above, the concept of *'ayb* extends almost over all domains of social interaction. It covers any infraction of the modesty code, filial and conjugal duty, proper behavior toward the community at large. It affects, then, the behavior of men, women, and children. Some of these domains are also controlled by the religious concept of *harām* (tabu), the violation of which brings *dhanb*. The latter includes many more domains than *'ayb*, but all the domains of the latter are included in the former, except for the domain of *wafa'*.

Both sets of key concepts discussed—*'ayb/dhanb* and *ghadab/rida*—reflect, on the ideological level, the fusion in Jiddah society of religious dogma and social norms. Two things need to be said about this fusion. First, the overlapping between the religious and the moral, the dogma and the social norms, that are embodied in the concepts endows them with great power. They have added force because not only is it a social but also a religious imperative to abide by the sanctions that they convey. Second, the fusion is not static. As I have argued earlier, ideologies change. Where customary behavior changes, a change in ideology is not far behind. The sinful deed becomes a shameless act. To sin, to incur *dhanb*, means to reject Allah's eternal authority. To act without shame means to violate a social norm which is not immutable. Conduct considered scandalous may now be improper at worst, or merely "modern" and, as such, indicative of things to come: regrettable, but apparently unavoidable.

How does this fusion affect ideational change? The data here suggest that when this fusion is combined with ambiguity in certain key concepts, it in fact facilitates ideational change. Ideational change is, of course, made further possible by contradictions which exist between the various concepts in the ideology and which, though obscured under some conditions, become apparent under new social circumstances. Harris suggests that ideational change results from incongruity between experience and ideology.[2] The data of this study further suggest that contradictions between various concepts in the ideology (as well as contradiction with experience) become—under changed conditions—a resource for ideational change. Different groups will stress different aspects of the ideology in their search to enhance their power. For example, a general principle of the ideology of *ahl al-balad* elite is seclusion. Yet, a contradiction exists in this principle. Seclusion of women, after all, has, as its converse, the exclusion of men. Thus the very seclusion "shielding" women from public life also excludes men from a domain affecting their public concerns. It is precisely this seclusion that gives women information about marriageable girls unavailable to the men but needed in the formation of kin groups.

As I argued earlier, the case of these families does not involve structural changes in their social behavior, their organizations, or their ideology. What we have here is a case of gradual, not dramatic, change in the relations of men to women and in filial relations. Seclusion of women and asymmetrical power relations between men and women, young and old, are reduced, but they are not transformed to full participation of women in public life, nor to an egalitarian distribution of power relations within domestic groups.

Similarly, the ideational change that has occurred was not a complete break with the current ideology but rather a working within its broad premises of male superiority and parental authority. This was possible through a modification of key concepts, secular and religious, and through the manipulation of one concept against another where contradiction existed in the ideology.

In saying that a modification in the concept of *'ayb* occurred, I maintain, as well, that *'ayb*, which includes a variety of behavioral domains, was redefined. One domain—that of *wafa'*—was excluded from *'ayb* behavior as it directly came to contradict another, more important domain: namely, honoring conjugal and filial duties. We have already seen the modification and redefinition of *'ayb* in connection with the specific issue of veiling. More generally, while obedience to husband is still enforced by *'ayb* and *dhanb* alike, the younger-generation women see this to be conditional upon perceived "reasonableness of his demands." The obvious ambiguity of such limits allows room for dissent and more freedom of action for wives who have not reached open defiance of their husbands' commands. Absolute obedience thus becomes qualified obedience, which, as has been shown, has allowed women, especially those who assume some aspects of male roles in the absence of their husbands, to overrule them in some decisions affecting their children.

Obligations of respect, obedience, and support to in-laws are still included in *'ayb* behavior (more than in *dhanb*), but they have been limited to allow greater freedom of action for the married couple. Again, this is done by giving priority to conjugal relations, which under conditions of neolocal residence have meant a considerable reduction of interference from in-laws in the daily lives of the conjugal pair.

Another domain of *'ayb* which was redefined relates to a woman's rights to her inheritance. Islamic law gives women the right to inherit half the measure of men. The concept of *'ayb* operated to cut a woman off from direct control of such property, as such control would imply distrust in her male kinsmen. When circumstances for women changed, so that now they have become educated and have more involvement in decisions affecting the family, woman have come to manipulate one domain (i.e., the social) in terms of the sacred. That is, it is not *'ayb* for a woman to want control of property since it is a right given by Allah. This contradiction between the sacred injunction and the social norm existed even for the older generation; but now it has been brought into the open to accommodate the new realities.

Another domain of *'ayb* which was redefined is related to contact between prospective marriage partners. As more and more alternative were sought to the older patterns, visual access or even prolonged socializing between the partners of the proposed marriage is no longer defined as *'ayb*. There is, however, ambiguity in how much contact is tolerated. Sayings attributed to the Prophet have often been quoted to validate this restriction in the domain of *'ayb* behavior. We see here an example that again demonstrates how, in this fusion of the moral and the religious, one level can be manipulated in terms of the other to validate the change in custom.

But *'ayb* also affects men's behavior. It is interesting that for a man *'ayb* and *dhanb* are still related to the behavior of his women, to honoring his duties as household head, to children, wife, dependents, parents, to "honest" business dealings. However, what is honest has sometimes been redefined in terms of what is expedient, given the recent increase in corruption accompanying economic transactions in the society. A man's duties to a wider circle of *arham* or to remote *ahl* are now dismissed as an ideal that cannot be realized.

This tendency is best understood in terms of increased geographic mobility, which has dispersed kin over many cities, and also in terms of the growth of the city of Jiddah, making new residential areas relatively more distant than in the past. People perceive this as a barrier, though they dismiss it when it comes to "closer relatives."

Similar processes have affected the concepts of *ghadab* and *rida,* which operated mainly in the field of parent-child relations. The ideology here still projects love from mother, support and discipline from father, gratitude and obedience from children. Such ideals had the backing of the key concept of *ghadab.*

As was shown earlier, *ghadab* encompasses a broad variety of parental reactions to children's delinquent behavior. The power of *ghadab* resides in the fusion of mystical and secular elements. To incur *ghadab* is to risk eternal damnation, as well as daily well-being. Those who observe their filial duty receive the *rida* of parents and of Allah. This *rida* is recompensed both in heaven and on earth, where the benefits include prosperity, well-being, and social harmony with kin and friends. Existing norms have been established by constant efforts to construct and reconstruct relations without incurring *ghadab.* But on the whole the ideology behind parent-child relations has not changed dramatically over the three generations. Minor changes occur to accommodate the emerging individuality of young men (as in their choice of career and spouse) and women (in their decision to continue their studies and defer marriage, in their right to veto a prospective groom, and in their relationships with their husbands).

Ghadab and *rida* also operate to maintain ideal relations between siblings, although the realities of inheritance today pose serious threats to such an ideal. While sibling relations used to be valued above material gain (and thus inhibited conflict in the family), today men and women alike place a great deal of importance upon their *rights* to property; for men, in order to maintain their position in the family and in society; for women, because property is a key to greater autonomy. Women particularly have begun to take full control over their property, even in the face of opposition by agnatic males. In validating such a breach with tradition, in confronting one domain of *'ayb* behavior, they fall back on their rights in Islam, as an inalienable *haqq* (right). Young men, too, dodge *'ayb* and *ghadab* in their desire for their rights of inheritance against older brothers or kinsmen.

All the above represent efforts at redefinitions of the limits that norms impose upon actors. It should be clear that social actors are constantly negotiating and renegotiating their social reality within the broad framework of what the ideology will allow. *Dhanb/'ayb* and *ghadab/rida*, as components of the ideology, have been reconstructed in such a way, then, that although they remain sanctions meant to deter or encourage, their ambiguities allow them to be applied in new ways. This development occurs over the long term, and much of it happens without conscious, deliberate planning on the part of the members of the domestic groups. But the final result is that standard meanings gain new currency. Ultimately, innovations occur largely as a result of the ability of men and women to adapt traditional and fundamental concepts to new circumstances.

In the light of all of the foregoing, while ideology is basically embedded in social relations, it is not an epiphenomenon of them, contra Durkheim. Nor, contra Marx, is it simply an epiphenomenon of productive relations. Being a blueprint, a template of reality, as Geertz holds, it organizes our experience, orients behavior, and makes prediction possible.[3] As Schlegel says:

> The decisions we make and the actions we take occur within the matrix of ideology. And how could it be otherwise? People do not form social groups and productive relations and then sit down to think and symbolize about them; rather, they act in accordance with both material and social advantage and the guiding principles that give the stamp of approval—or disapproval—to their actions. For this reason, ideology, to whatever degree it traces its origins to material or social relations, must be treated as an independent variable in the exploration of sexual status.[4]

Thus, we recognize that the above changes in the ideology have occurred in consequence of changes in social relations. And we also recognize that ideology has acted upon these relations and shaped them. Throughout, the discussion has shown how, on the one hand, ideology has worked effectively to maintain asymmetrical power distribution between men and women and old and young, thereby maintaining hierarchical differentiation and, in a sense, validating this distribution of power. At the same time, when power relations between men and women changed in consequence of new circumstances, I have shown how the ideology was manipulated to accommodate this distribution of power between the sexes.

Another theoretical point concerning the ideology of *ahl al-balad* elite is the mutuality of relationship between it and the behavior of the men and women in these groups. If in the past the ideology stressed absolute obedience of women to their husband's wishes, women have begun to question the limits of their husband's power over them, especially when his power is expressed in physical violence and whimsical restrictions of movement. At the same time, wives, especially the younger ones, make greater demands upon their husbands' time than their mothers ever dared or had to, given the changing patterns of postnuptial residence.

Concerning ideology acting on behavior as an independent variable, the following two examples illustrate the point well. In spite of her right to veto a proposed marriage, a girl has still no chance to pursue her own interests or follow her own sentiments, given the barriers to heterosexual contacts. Nor is it possible for a woman who can support herself to live alone, as such an arrangement militates against the presumption of male dominance—be it couched in terms of protection or in terms of Islamic teachings.

Another point about ideology is that research has revealed that ideologies are often distortions of social reality, rather than accurate reflections of it. Ideologies may underscore one aspect of experience and ignore another[5] or even be social structures in reverse[6] and quite contrary to social reality.[7] Yet, the present study tends to show that a greater congruence exists between the ideology and the reality than the literature suggests and that the principles of social organization recall the axioms of the domestic ideology of these groups.[8]

Beyond these considerations, it is important to stress the malleability of the ideology of domestic groups. Groups will seek to utilize those parts of the ideology—leaving untouched other aspects of it—which can be invoked to benefit their interests.[9] In this respect it is fitting to view the behavior of individuals in terms of their strategies, which represent efforts at reinterpreting ideological imperatives.

To begin with, an understanding of human behavior that refers merely to community ideological norms will be incomplete. That is not to say that norms are not relevant. After all, people may fail to observe the norms but act in reference to them.[10] Even where they ignore the norms, they refrain from open defiance of them, and, by such acquiescence, make them official.[11] Some conform to the norms because conformity brings them prestige. Within the constraints of the norms, or even in using these norms, men and women alike are not pawns but are actively involved in strategies that further their own interests. Some of these strategies aim at producing "regular practices"—a legitimating strategy that aims at making the egoistic interests appear to be the public interest.[12]

These ideas are not new. Anthropologists have revealed that individuals do not fall into cultural molds prescribed by societal norms but actually manipulate and use them to their own advantage.[13] Arguing beyond this, we must recall that there is no universal logic to seeking advantage and that people's competition for advantage is a product of their interpretation of the world and those in it. Research has also shown that people, though constrained by "normative rules," also have "pragmatic ones." Both are used in the "stratagems" of men to attain their spoils.[14] Hence, rules may themselves become resources on which people draw to achieve egoistic ends.[15] This, in fact, is one of the arguments made by Caroline Bledsoe's study of Kpelle society, where she demonstrates that men, as well as women, draw on the norms when it is expedient to do so in order to advance their political power.[16]

My findings are similar. Some norms are clearly endorsed by religious ideology, and these are perhaps the most difficult to flout or defy. However, in actuality people do not strictly observe them. Veiling is a case in point. As I have shown in chapter 2 behavior and norms have changed, but even when the norms change, women, in their attempts to gain more relative autonomy, have varied in their observance of them. Men, too, were not in total observance of 'ayb and *ghadab* sanctions. Like women, they have modified these key concepts to accommodate their incipient independence from parental control and from obligations to a wide network of kin, especially *arham*.

The actual behavior of younger-generation women did not conform to the norms of reciprocity governing *wafa'* (either social visits or exchange of gifts) as their interest shifted from friendship networks to conjugal relations, which today afford them relative security.

Within the household the strategies of women have been to engage in a process of reordering the heirarchy of meanings encompassed in the norms. The result, they hope, will be more autonomy, more control of the budget, more involvement in decisions regarding their children and the family as a whole, the right to veto the decisions of agnates on marriage, and, finally, greater control of their property. Many of these strategies were inspired by and in turn affected a modified definition of women's role in the family and her relationship to her spouse and agnates. All these strategies resulted in relatively more power for women, and, as such, they must be seen as aimed at political ends.[17]

Even for the older generation, where norms of seclusion for women were more restrictive of women's mobility and the resultant dependency on men was greater, women invested time, energy, and money in sustaining networks of friendship with other women in other households. They thereby widened their social horizons and reduced the precariousness of their status in society.[18] The strategies here involved cooperation with other women and provided women with information vital to both men and women but actually controlled exclusively by women.[19]

Because of the limitations of fieldwork, this study has concentrated on women's strategies more than those of men, especially in the public arena. However, within the domestic group and sometimes also outside it (as in marriage choices) I delineated the strategies of the two as similar in goals, if not in means.

If we consider marriage, for example, the regularities observed could not simply be explained as a preference to marry patrilateral cousins or a more general restriction of marriage to a narrow circle of relatives and *arham*. Whereas jural and moral incentives cannot be discounted, these regularities become intelligible when seen as also the result of pragmatic consideration by men and women.

From this perspective I examined both continuity and change in marriages among these families. In making marriage choices for their sons and daughters men aim to increase and maintain the economic and symbolic capital of the *'a'ilah.* The strategies of women are guided by their own interest in preserving smooth relations in the household by selecting a woman who would neither threaten the authority distribution within the domestic group nor make extravagant demands on its budget.

Bourdieu's penetrating analysis of matrimonial strategies among the Kabyles uncovers a similar phenomenon in Algeria. Though in both cases the ultimate decision on marriage transactions rests with men, the Jiddah elite woman clearly has, through her strict seclusion, more room to maneuver for her interests than her counterpart among the Kabyles. Since these interests relate indirectly to the cohesion of the domestic group by crossing the first line of fission between women in the extended family (and, by the same logic, to the second line of fission between wives of sons), these strategies are also related to the common interest of the *'a'ilah.* Further, as sometimes happens in the Kabyles case, they are not opposed by men.[20]

It is clearly in this light that one must understand the changes in marriage over the three generations in this study. Despite increasing changes allowing for more individual choice, marriage remains an agreement between families. The links between *arhum* structure cooperation, both economic and social; determine status for the offspring from the marriage; affect prestige by either maintaining, expanding, or diminishing it for the families involved. Hence the continuity of marriage arrangements in the face of changing conditions. For, as Bourdieu has argued in the case of the Kabyles, these ensure the reproduction of the system: they preserve and increase the economic and symbolic capital of the families, and thus they tend to reproduce the relations or conditions that made them possible.[21]

Sometimes, however, women's interests cannot be subsumed by those of men. Indeed, in trying to get more control over their lives, women's strategies may conflict with the interests of their men. The concepts of *'ayb* and *dhanb* reduce the tension by favoring the authority of men. But, as I indicated earlier, these key concepts are being modified, and one can expect that for the fourth generation the tension may grow to a direct conflict of interests. This prediction, however, must be tempered by the importance of kinship ideology in the culture as a whole.

Thus, if we look at property relations, they are still primarily dominated by men. Studies in other Middle Eastern societies have suggested that a control of her property can only be attained by forfeiting a woman's kin rights.[22] These reports, however, reduce kinship to mere property relations, ignoring the ideological basis of kin obligations in a society where a woman's conduct is connected to the honor of her natal family.

My data show that a woman may assert her rights to her property or transfer its control to her husband without jeopardizing her relations with her natal family, provided that these relations do not suffer strain prior to the decision and if the discussions themselves end in an amicable agreement. Women's rights to property are endorsed by Islam—a matter which young women use to legitimate their break with tradition and to evade censure by *'ayb*. Although there is no de facto control of property by women in these families, the indications are that women are becoming assertive in seeking such control.

As a final note, it may be recalled that the basic aim of this book was to study continuity and change in the ideology and social organization of domestic groups in an urban Saudi society. There is a tendency by observers of internal developments in Saudi Arabia to stress elements of fixity in the culture and in social relations. This research shows that such an ahistorical perspective is misleading. Although many factors of continuity have been discussed, significant change has occurred in the ideology and practice of the domestic groups under investigation. We cannot know what the patterns of relationships will be in the future. But the changes that have already occurred will not easily be reversed. Thus, the fourth generation of women will be the inheritors of the reinterpretations of ideology and modifications of social relations that have been examined here. It will be fascinating to observe how they deal with them as they grow into mature adults.

NOTES

1. One cannot claim that the women are not to some extent autonomous. In fact, their very segregation makes such autonomy possible, as women

conduct their daily lives with other women independently of men. Lloyd A. Fallers and Margaret C. Fallers, in "Sex Roles in Edremit," observed a similar situation in Turkey.

2. Nigel Harris, *Beliefs in Society*, p. 28.

3. Clifford Geertz, "Ideology as a Cultural System."

4. Schlegel, ed., *Sexual Stratification*, p. 35.

5. Olivia Harris, "Complementarity and Conflicts."

6. Philip Carl Salzman, "Ideology and Change in Middle Eastern Tribal Societies."

7. Stanley Brandes, "Like Wounded Stags."

8. Recent research by feminist anthropologists has pointed to the relevance of further differentiation in the analysis of ideology. One cannot assume consensus on the whole of the ideology, according to this research. In fact, studies of this sort have clearly shown the differentiation of the sexes on the cultural construction of gender (Y. Murphy and R. F. Murphy, *Women of the Forest*) and pointed to the implications of such differentiation for social change (Daisy Hilse Dwyer, "Ideologies of Sexual Inequality and Strategies for Change"). This study, however, was not specifically concerned with cultural constructions of gender; moreover, as explained earlier, it draws more of the data from women than from men.

9. The plasticity of ideology has been shown through the research of Geertz, "Ideology as a Cultural System," Abdalla Bujra, *The Politics of Stratification*, Johnson, *Islam and the Politics of Meaning*, and others.

10. See Johnson, *Islam and the Politics of Meaning*.

11. Bourdieu, *Outline of a Theory of Practice*, p. 40.

12. *Ibid.*

13. See Max Gluckman, *Politics, Law, and Ritual in Tribal Society;* Meyer Fortes, "Introduction," in Meyer Fortes, ed., *Marriage in Tribal Societies;* and F. G. Bailey, *Stratagems and Spoils.*

14. See Bailey, *Stratagems and Spoils.*

15. See Norman E. Whitten and Dorothea S. Whitten, "Social Strategies and Social Relationships."

16. See Caroline H. Bledsoe, *Women and Marriage in Kpelle Society.*

17. Political is here defined in reference to the distribution of power and decisions in society.

18. I have argued elsewhere (see Altorki, "Religion and Social Organization") that such networks tend to occur with women's seclusion.

19. Research has also revealed that women may compete against other women. In their effort to attain more control, older women use younger ones. See, for example, Bledsoe, *Women and Marriage in Kpelle Society.* In fact, as Collier points out, women's conflict is itself a strategy to attain political ends. For this view see Jane Fishburne Collier, "Women in Politics."

20. Bourdieu, *Outline of a Theory*, pp. 44–46.

21. *Ibid.*, p. 70.

22. See Harry Rosenfeld, "On Determinants of the Status of Arab Village Women," and Safia Mohsen, "Aspects of the Legal Status of Women Among Awlad 'Ali."

Glossary

'aba' A black cloak worn over the dress and covering the entire body.

ahadith (sing., *hadith*) Sayings attributed to the Prophet, Muhammad.

ahl An unbounded bilateral kin group.

ahl al-balad Literally, "people of the country." A demographic concept used by people to differentiate themselves from the foreign community, from recent immigrants, and also from Bedouin tribes. The concept establishes fluid boundaries between groups.

'a'ilah People who share common agnatic descent and thus belong to the same patrilineage.

ujanib (sing. *ajnabi*) Literally, "foreigners." It also refers to friends with whom a measure of social distance is observed.

arham Affinal relatives who are married into ego's *ahl* and ego's spouse's *ahl*.

'aql Reason, rationality, understanding, judicious judgment. [*'aqilah*: a woman possessing *'aql*.]

Ashraf (sing. Sharif) A local dynasty which ruled the Hijaz in the early part of the twentieth century and was overthrown by 'Abd al-'Aziz ibn Sa'ud in 1925.

'ayb Shame.

badu (sing. *badawi*) Nomad.

baqshish A money donation made to singers and/or dancers on festive occasions, especially marriage.

bashkat	A crony network that meets regularly. It is similar to the Iranian institution known as a *dawrah*.
dhanb	Sin. Covers the operational aspect of *harām*, *q.v.* (one incurs *dhanb* when one commits *harām*) and also a wider sphere of undesirable behavior.
faqihah	An informal girl's school. It taught the Qur'an, needlework, and some arithmetic.
fitnah	Disorder, chaos; also, an alluringly beautiful woman; the charm, enchantment, and fascination associated with a *femme fatale*.
ghadab	Anger, wrath.
hajj	The pilgrimage to Macca.
haqq Allah	That which rightfully belongs to Allah, or Allah's dues.
harām	Tabu. Forbidden by Islamic injunctions. (See also *dhanb*.)
haram	The Holy Mosque in Macca.
Hijazi	A person from the Hijaz, the province in which are located the holy cities of Macca and Madina.
istiqamah	A term connoting proper social and religious behavior.
'itab	Censure, blame, reproof, reprimand. As used by the people, the term refers to a process of expressing disappointment without necessarily resorting to show of anger or insult.
khal	Mother's brother. [*khawal*, maternal kin.]
khirah	Divination.
ma'dhun shar'i	A religious specialist who draws up the marriage contract; he may also issue a divorce.
mahr	A payment due to the wife from her husband upon her marriage.

mahram (pl. *maharim*)	A male relative whom a woman cannot marry; being in a degree of consanguinity or affinity precluding marriage.
mawalid	Offspring of marriages between slaves and nonslaves.
muqata'ah	Indifference, separation, break with someone. As used by the people, it refers to a condition of severing all relations between two or more parties.
mutawwif (pl. *mutawwifin*)	An agent for the servicing of the needs of pilgrims.
Najdite	A person from Najd, the province in the central highlands of Saudi Arabia where the capital city, Riyadh, is located.
nifs	A concept used in Morocco to refer to the desires of the flesh.
qadi	A judge who administers *shari'ah* law.
qismah	Destiny, fate (foreordained by Allah).
rami	Gifts of gold and jewelry specifically given at childbirth.
rida	Contentment, satisfaction.
sadaqah	Alms-giving, charity.
shari'ah	The Islamic legal code.
Shuruq	A term referring to people from Najd (see Najdite).
sudqan	Close friends, usually among women.
sulh	Reconciliation; literally, "peace."
takruni	An African.
tarawih	A special prayer performed during Ramadan.
tarhah	A chiffon shawl draped around the head and covering the face.
tawkil	A delegation of proxy.
'uddah	A condition of tabu observance which a Muslim woman enters upon the death of

	her husband. It lasts four months and ten days.
'ulama'	The men learned in the religious law.
'umrah	The minor pilgrimage performed in the Holy Mosque in Macca.
wafa'	A term that refers to the pattern of social visits between women and the resultant ties of mutual support and assistance. It also refers to gifts and favors exchanged between friends (male and female).
wakil	Deputy; guardian.
wali	A representative of Ottoman rule in Jiddah and Macca in the period before the establishment of the kingdom.
wufyan	Formal friends, usually used by women.
wu'ud	Formal visits exchanged by women.
zakat (al-mal)	A Muslim religious tax of 2½ percent on capital and earnings.

Bibliography

Altorki, Soraya. "The Anthropologist in the Field: A Case of 'Indigenous Anthropology' from Saudi Arabia." In Hussein Fahim, ed., *Indigenous Anthropology in Non-Western Countries.* Durham, N.C.: Carolina Academic Press, 1982.

——"Family Organization and Women's Power in Urban Saudi Arabian Society." *Journal of Anthropological Research* (1977) 33:277–87.

——"Religion and Social Organization of Elite Families in Urban Saudi Arabia." Ph.D. diss., University of California, Berkeley, 1973.

Altorki, Soraya, Klaus Friedrich-Koch, Andrew Arno, and Letitia Hickson. "Ritual Reconciliation and the Obviation of Grievances: A Comparative Study in the Ethnography of Law." *Ethnology* (1977) 16:269–84.

Al-Ansari, 'Abd al-Quddus. *Ta'rikh Madinat Jiddah.* Jiddah: Asfahani Press, 1963.

Atkinson, Jane Monning. "Review Essay: Anthropology." *Signs* (1982) 8:236–58.

Antoun, Richard. "On the Modesty of Women in Arab Muslim Villages: A Study in the Accommodation of Traditions." *American Anthropologist* (1968) 70:671–97.

Bailey, F. G. *Stratagems and Spoils: A Social Anthropology of Politics.* New York: Schocken Books, 1969.

Baqasi, 'Ayishah bint 'Abdullah. *Bilad al-Hijaz fi al-'Asr al-Ayyubi, 576–648 A.H.* [1171–1250 A.D.]. Macca: Dar Macca li al-Tiba'ah wa al-Nashr, 1980.

Barclay, Harold B. *Burri al-Lamaab: A Suburban Village in the Sudan.* Ithaca, N.Y.: Cornell University Press, 1964.

Bendix, Reinhard. *Max Weber: An Intellectual Portrait.* Garden City, N.Y.: Anchor Books, 1962.

Berreman, Gerald. *Hindus of the Himalayas.* Berkeley: University of California Press, 1963.

Bledsoe, Caroline H. *Women and Marriage in Kpelle Society.* Stanford, Calif.: Stanford University Press, 1980.

Bott, Elizabeth. *Family and Social Networks.* London: Tavistock, 1971.

Bourdieu, Pierre. *Outline of a Theory of Practice.* New York: Cambridge University Press, 1977.

Brandes, Stanley. "Like Wounded Stags: Male Sexual Ideology in an Andalusian Town." In Sherry B. Ortner and Harriet Whitehead, eds., *Sexual Meanings: The Cultural Construction of Gender and Sexuality.* Cambridge: Cambridge University Press, 1981.

Bujra, Abdalla. *The Politics of Stratification.* London: Oxford University Press, 1971.

Burton, Sir Richard F. *A Personal Narrative of a Pilgrimage to AL-Madinah & Meccah.* 1855. Reprint, New York: Dover Books, 1964.

Caufield, Mina Davis. "Equality, Sex and the Mode of Production." In Gerald D. Berreman and Kathleen M. Zaretsky, eds., *Social Inequality: Comparative and Developmental Approaches.* New York: Academic Press, 1981.

Chodorow, N. "Family Structure and Feminine Personality." In Michelle Rosaldo and Louise Lamphere, eds., *Women, Culture, and Society.* Stanford, Calif.: Stanford University Press, 1974.

Cohen, Abner. *Arab Border Villages in Israel: A Study of Continuity and Change in Social Organization.* Manchester: Manchester University Press, 1965.

Collier, Jane Fishburne. "Women in Politics." In Michelle Zimbalist Rosaldo and Louise Lamphere, eds., *Women, Culture, and Society.* Stanford, Calif.: Stanford University Press, 1974.

Collier, Jane Fishburne and Michelle Z. Rosaldo. "Politics and Gender in Simple Societies." In Sherry B. Ortner and Harriet Whitehead, eds., *Sexual Meanings: The Cultural Construction of Gender and Sexuality.* Cambridge: Cambridge University Press, 1981.

Dwyer, Daisy Hilse. "Ideologies of Sexual Inequality and Strategies for Change in Male-Female Relations." *American Ethnologist* (1978) 5:227–40.

—— *Images and Self-Images: Male and Female in Morocco.* New York: Columbia University Press, 1978.

English, Paul Ward. *City and Village in Iran: Settlements and Economy in the Kirman Basin.* Milwaukee: University of Wisconsin Press, 1966.

Esposito, John L. *Women in Muslim Family Law.* Syracuse, N.Y.: Syracuse University Press, 1982.

Fallers, Lloyd A. and Margaret C. Fallers. "Sex Roles in Edremit." In J. G. Peristiany, ed., *Mediterranean Family Structures.* Cambridge: Cambridge University Press, 1976.

Fortes, Meyer. "Introduction." In Meyer Fortes, ed., *Marriage in Tribal Societies.* Cambridge: Cambridge University Press, 1962.

Friedl, Ernestine. *Women and Men: An Anthropologist's View.* New York: Holt, Rinehart and Winston, 1975.

Geertz, Clifford. "Ideology as a Cultural System." In David Apter, ed., *Ideology and Discontent.* New York: Free Press, 1964.

Geertz, Clifford, Hildred Geertz, and Lawrence Rosen. *Meaning and Order in Moroccan Society: Three Essays in Cultural Analysis.* Cambridge: Cambridge University Press, 1979.

Giddens, Anthony. *Capitalism and Modern Social Theory.* Cambridge: Cambridge University Press, 1971.

Gluckman, Max. *Politics, Law, and Ritual in Tribal Society.* Chicago: Aldine, 1965.

Goldrup, Lawrence P. "Saudi Arabia, 1902–1932." Ph.D. diss., UCLA, 1971.

Harris, Nigel. *Beliefs in Society.* London: Watts, 1968.

Harris, Olivia. "Complementarity and Conflicts." In J. S. LaFontaine, ed., *Sex and Age as Principles of Sexual Differentiation.* Association of Social Anthropologists, Monograph 17. New York: Academic Press, 1978.

Hurgronje, Snouck. *Mekka in the Later Part of the Nineteenth Century.* 1885–89. Reprint, Leiden: E. J. Brill, 1970.

Izutsu, Toshihiko. *Ethico-Religious Concepts in the Quran.* Montreal: McGill University Press, 1966.

Jacobson, Doranne. "Hidden Faces: Hindu and Muslim Purdah in a Central Indian Village." Ph.D. diss., Columbia University, 1970.

Johnson, Nels. *Islam and the Politics of Meaning in Palestinian Nationalism.* London: Kegan Paul International, 1982.

Leacock, Eleanor Burke. "Introduction to Frederick Engels." In Friedrich Engels, *The Origin of the Family, Private Property, and the State,* ed. Eleanor Burke Leacock. New York: International Publishers, 1972.

Mernissi, Fatima. *Beyond the Veil: Male Female Dynamics in a Modern Muslim Society.* New York: Schenkman, 1975.

Mohsen, Safia. "Aspects of the Legal Status of Women Among Awlad 'Ali." *Anthropological Quarterly* (1967) 40:153–66.

Murphy, Y. and R. F. Murphy. *Women of the Forest.* New York: Columbia University Press, 1974.

Nash, June. "The Aztecs and the Ideology of Male Dominance." *Signs* (1978) 4:349–62.

Ortner, Sherry B. "Is Female to Male as Nature is to Culture?" In Michelle Zimbalist Rosaldo and Louise Lamphere, eds., *Women, Culture, and Society.* Stanford, Calif.: Stanford University Press, 1974.

Ortner, Sherry B. and Harriet Whitehead. "Introduction: Accounting for Sexual Meanings." In Sherry B. Ortner and Harriet B. Whitehead, eds., *Sexual Meanings: The Cultural Construction of Gender.* Cambridge: Cambridge University Press, 1981.

Papanek, Hanna. "Purdah: Separate Worlds and Symbolic Shelter." In Hannah Papanek and Gail Minault, eds., *Separate Worlds: Studies of Purdah in South Asia.* Delhi: Chanayka, 1982.

Peters, Emrys. "Aspects of Rank and Status Among Muslims in a Lebanese Village." In Pitt Rivers, ed., *Mediterranean Countrymen.* Paris: Mouton, 1963.

Rapp, Rayner. "Review Essay: Anthropology." *Signs* (1979) 4:497–513.

Rentz, George. "Wahhabism and Saudi Arabia." In Derek Hopwood, ed., *The Arabian Peninsula: Society and Politics.* London: Allen and Unwin, 1972.

Rogers, Susan Carol. "Female Forms of Power and the Myth of Male Dominance: A Model of Female/Male Interaction in Peasant Society." *American Ethnologist* (1975) 2:741–54.

Rosaldo, Michelle Zimbalist. "The Use and Abuse of Anthropology: Reflections on Feminism and Cross Cultural Understanding." *Signs* (1980) 5:389–417.

—— "Women, Culture, and Society: A Theoretical Overview." In Michelle Zimbalist Rosaldo and Louise Lamphere, eds., *Women, Culture, and Society.* Stanford, Calif.: Stanford University Press, 1974.

Rosenfeld, Harry. "On Determinants of the Status of Arab Village Women." *Man* (1960) 60:66–81.

Rubin, Gayle. "The Traffic in Women: Notes on the 'Political Economy' of Sex." In Rayna R. Reiter, ed., *Toward an Anthropology of Women*. New York: Monthly Review Press, 1975.

Sacks, Karen. "Engels Revistited: Woman, the Organization of Production, and Private Property." In Michelle Zimbalist Rosaldo and Louise Lamphere, eds., *Women, Culture, and Society*. Stanford, Calif.: Stanford University Press, 1974.

Salzman, Philip Carl. "Ideology and Change in Middle Eastern Tribal Societies." *Man* (1978) 13:618–37.

Sanday, Peggy. *Female Power and Male Dominance*. Cambridge: Cambridge University Press, 1981.

Schlegel, Alice, ed. *Sexual Stratification: A Cross-Cultural View*. New York: Columbia University Press, 1977.

Siba'i, Ahmad. *Ta'rikh Macca: Dirasat fi al-Siyasah wa al-'Ilm wa al-Ijtima' wa al-'Umran*. Vol. 1, 2d ed. Macca: Dar Quraysh, 1960.

——— *Ta'rikh Macca: Dirasat fi al-Siyasah wa al-'Ilm wa al-Ijtima' wa al-'Umran*. Vol. 2, 3d ed. Macca: Dar Quraysh, 1965.

Spiro, Melford E. *Children of the Kibbutz*. New York: Schocken Books, 1958.

Whitten, Norman E. and Dorothea S. Whitten. "Social Strategies and Social Relationships." *Annual Review of Anthropology* (1972) 1:247–70.

Yalman, Nur. "On the Purity of Women in the Castes of Ceylon and Malaber." *Journal of the Royal Anthropological Institute* (1963) 93:25–58.

Yanagisaro, Sylvia Junko. "Family and Household: The Analysis of Domestic Groups." *Annual Review of Anthropology* (1979) 8:161–205.

Index